RAINBOWS OVER RUINS

SUSAN SHERAYKO

RAINBOWS OVER RUINS

SUSAN SHERAYKO

ARPress

ILLUMINATING IDEAS
EMPOWERING VOICES

ARPress
45 Dan Road Suite 5
Canton MA 02021
Hotline: 1(888) 821-0229
Fax: 1(508) 545-7580

Ordering Information:
Quantity sales. Special discounts are available on quantity purchases by corporations, associations, and others. For details, contact the publisher at the address above.

Printed in the United States of America.

ISBN-13:   Paperback   979-8-89389-000-6
            eBook   979-8-89389-002-0
            Hardback   979-8-89389-001-3

Library of Congress Control Number: 2023900143

"A modern-day *Siddhartha*. *Rainbows Over Ruins* walks you through a spiritual journey that is not focused on the 'out there' but more on the 'in here.' How do we transition from one phase of our lives while allowing ourselves to grow from what we have learned from the past? Susan helps you help yourself."

Wileen Charles, Founder, Starseed Foundation

"Susan has an amazing ability to help me gain clarity and focus about the possibilities that surround me. Susan is so skilled and supportive that her faith in my abilities has transformed my thinking, and now I know the action steps I want to take with certainty and enthusiasm."

Susan Prime, Prime Coaching, United Kingdom

"Susan uses her whole brain when crafting solutions. She knows how to visualize the results she wants and then build the structure to support the dream. She constantly prods people who are stuck in one way of seeing something into realizing new paths to climb up the mountain of success. Now she is willing to share her unique approach to creating success systems with people who are ready to go to the next level in their business and personal lives."

Kate Maxwell, Hypnotherapist, Spiritual Life Coach

"Calm, serenity, wisdom, patience, empathy—these are the characteristics that I think of when I think of Susan. Throughout our relationship, she has always shared openly and freely with me. Susan has never been judgmental (of anyone really) or unkind with words. She has an amazing ability to take in all the information surrounding a situation, process it in a kind, loving, and logical way, and then interpret the information back in such a way that I feel I too can learn and grow from the experience… whether it was mine or not. I believe that Susan is a conduit… maybe not the right word… a channel… okay, in laymen's terms, she is the glue that holds us all together. If I were in crisis… I'd want Susan to be with me more than anyone I know."

Toni Casala, Owner, Children in Film

"What I appreciate about Susan is her sincere and great generosity of spirit. She has an almost unlimited tolerance for the foibles of others and manages to find humor in some of the most trying circumstances. I can always count on Susan to give me an honest, balanced assessment of whatever is happening privately or globally. She never stagnates. She's always seeking ways to make her life better and more meaningful. That is inspirational to me."

Susan Scudder, Actress, Casting Director

To my dear husband, Peter, who has faced the challenge to choose rainbows over ruins as my trusty sidekick.

It's not your work to make anything happen. It's your work to dream it and let it happen. *Law of Attraction* will make it happen. In your joy, you create something, and then you maintain your vibrational harmony with it, and the universe must find a way to bring it about. That's the promise of *Law of Attraction*.

—Abraham (nonphysical intelligence

expressed through author Esther Hicks)

CONTENTS

APPENDIXES

FOREWORD

BY NOAH ST. JOHN

As the inventor of Afformations®, I receive e-mails, phone calls, postcards, and social media messages every day about how my Afformations method has changed people's lives. (As you will read in this book, Afformations are empowering questions that immediately change your subconscious beliefs from negative to positive.)

Of course, I'm truly humbled by every Afformations success story and delighted to hear all of the amazing results people are getting with this method. And naturally, some stories tend to stick in the memory more than others.

For example, I remember one particular story about a woman who lived in California who was in serious credit card debt and, in her own words, "ducking calls from creditors" because she couldn't pay her bills. After a friend told her about my work and Afformations, this woman told me that she started to use my four-step Afformations method that I describe in my books and online programs, and that her life began to change for the better as a result.

She then proceeded to tell me how, in less than six months, she had gone from tens of thousands of dollars in debt to a six-figure income as a result of learning how to change her subconscious beliefs using Afformations.

This remarkable woman, as you've no doubt guessed by now, is none other than the author of the book you're holding, Susan Sherayko.

As I've gotten to know Susan as a client and friend, it's clear that she has not only done the inner work we all must do to overcome our own individual roadblocks and hurdles; she is now leading the way for many other people to follow in her footsteps.

In short, Susan is lighting the way for a whole new group of Afformers—that's what we call ourselves, folks who use Afformations! It's my privilege to write the foreword for Susan's new book, Rainbows Over Ruins, because it tells the extraordinary true story of how Susan took circumstances that would have derailed the average person and turned them into stepping-stones to triumph.

Of course, Susan is not the average person—and neither are you.

That's why you're holding this book right now.

If you are facing adversity or hardship, if you want to overcome the pain of the past, I urge you to use the wisdom in this book to help you light the way to a better future.

Until we meet…

Happy reading and keep afforming!

Noah St. John
Inventor of Afformations® and author,
The Book of Afformations®
www.NoahStJohn.com

PREFACE

THE LANDSLIDE

The morning of February 5, 2005, seemed like any other day. It was raining, as it had been for several days, as I headed off to the studio. We were wrapping a major production of *A Place of Our Own* and its sister show in Spanish, *Los Ninos en su Casa,* for KCET in California. As production manager, I felt we had accomplished an amazing feat: ten episodes a week, for a total of 220 episodes in six months. It felt gratifying that the program could contribute so much to the early child- care providers charged with preparing preschoolers for kindergarten.

Crew and talent were tired and looking forward to the hiatus that inevitably follows an intense production. Time is such a precious commodity when we're involved in a show. The host of the Spanish episodes, Alina R., had just been talking to me about how much she was looking forward to a little downtime to clean out her kitchen drawers. I heartily concurred with her. I had projects like that in mind as well. My husband, Peter, and I had just lifted the corner of carpeting in our dining room to see whether we would be refinishing hardwood floors or replacing carpeting.

I loved our stucco house of the 1930s, with its plaster walls, beehive fireplace, and D&M Malibu tiles leading to the second story. Located in Los Angeles in the Verdugo Hills, the house was actually built into the mountain wall, which rose at a sharp slope behind it. The original builder had the forethought to use steel pillars back in the 1930s, which had proven valuable in earthquake country. Nothing rattled this house. When we sat on the patio, we could see rocky outcroppings above us, yet we never felt any concern. The house and mountain were comfortable, nestled away from the bustle of the city. With the mountain behind us and a storm reservoir out front, our nearest neighbors were a half mile west and a tenth of a mile east.

Pipe corrals for our horses covered our entire front yard along the street, not unlike other Los Angeles homes. We thought of it as a ranch, although at less than 10,000 square feet, it definitely fell into the postage-stamp category. Most important to us, it allowed us to enjoy the trappings of the western lifestyle that Peter found so important, even if we had outgrown the space and every project undertaken seemed massive.

An actor and Western aficionado, Peter had been growing a home-based business, renting the things that make Westerns authentic. Everything was stored at home, in every nook and cranny—the garage, the patio, a small basement, the living room, the dining room, and an upstairs bedroom. It was the kind of business that worked well out of our home but could easily flounder with the addition of overhead on top of living expenses. We wanted to locate a larger ranch but had no idea how it was possible. We frequently joked that we would have to move before we could sell the house. We couldn't possibly stage it for potential buyers when it was filled with so much old stuff.

Driving through the congested streets and highways toward the studio just south of Los Feliz that morning, there was nothing out of the ordinary happening. Peter was heading off to Arizona for Winter Range, the second largest annual cowboy action shooting event in the United States. I was anticipating a trip to Seattle during break to see my amazing grandson, Charlie, and shower him with gifts, even if my daughter Amy and son-in-law Tom might not be all that enthusiastic about my spoiling him.

There were plenty of tensions between the members of the producing team. For the past nine months, we had struggled to keep our heads wrapped around the sheer volume of logistics and creative components involved, hard-pressed to support one another. We all wanted to feel that someone had our back so that the paranoia associated with potential failure would go away, but the stress was undermining even the best relationships.

Although Peter and I had accomplished a modest track record in the entertainment industry, making a living was project-based. There was always an ongoing search to maintain current production activity, along with a goal to build enough residual income to sustain us during the unknown time period between projects. It added an element of continual uncertainty about when and where to spend money—with the result that we often found we had no time to enjoy spending when we were working and little to spend when we were between shows.

Peter had a few notable screen credits; his role of Texas Jack in *Tombstone* made him a recognizable figure in his community. His book *Tombstone: The Guns and Gear* had been released to high critical praise, and the first edition was selling out. His company Caravan West had grown since the film's release and had a healthy roster of credits. Peter had even rebounded from a staggering horse wreck and gone on to appear in a one-man show, *Cody: An Evening with Buffalo Bill,* which had been presented in chautauquas in Ohio and Germany.

Not as public, I had my own passions on two fronts. An actor turned businessperson, I too was immersed in the entertainment industry. I had been named one of the top 250 women in the industry by *Business of Film Magazine* while involved in international sales, had earned my MBA, and had been honored with a service award from the Producers Guild of America for my work as chairperson of the seminar committee for several years.

My other passion was more private. I was and am a seeker, someone who not only searches for knowledge of a higher self but also desires to share that knowledge with others, who may improve their lives and achieve life-enhancing results from that awareness. Raised a Presbyterian, during subsequent years, I studied the works of philosopher Rudolf Steiner, was ordained a deacon in the Gnostic tradition, received certificates as a psychosynthesis trainer (a transpersonal psychology), and participated in the meditations of the International Foundation for Integral Psychology, founded by Dr. Robert Gerard. However, the unfortunate circumstances surrounding the death of my long-standing mentor Vivian King in 2000 set me on my heels. It was a dark night of the soul, during which I turned to the church of my upbringing. And as I got into the car that morning, I was serving as the deacon moderator at church.

At the studio, a pretty routine wrap was underway. News coverage indicated several troubled areas near my home—traffic lights out and street flooding—but when my line producer Ellen R. asked me if I needed to go home, I thought I would be fine. Since Peter would be away, I was in no hurry to get home.

Even the drive back that night was nondescript, except for traffic delays. I stopped at the grocery store to stock up for the weekend before heading to the house. Getting out of the car, I didn't notice anything out of place. There was a different smell in the air, but in the combination of horses, mud, and rain, there was nothing that alarmed me. As I approached the house in the dark, some white sand stood out on the sidewalk, not terribly threatening after so much rain.

I had no idea as I turned the key in the lock and flipped the light switch that night that what I would see before me would turn out to be a life-altering event. The mind takes in and tries to process so many images when it doesn't recognize what is in front of it. The dogs were all on the sofas, wagging their tails to say, "Hi, Mom." Mud was all around them and down the stairs from the second floor, and water dripped from the ceiling below the upstairs bathroom. I ran up the stairs, through the mud, to find a wall of dirt and stone had pushed through the upstairs windows, across the hall, and into the bathroom, where six inches of dark brown water filled the tiled floor.

I freaked, running around, trying to reach Peter. "You've got to come home *now*." We needed help. None of our friends were available. Fortunately, Max from the church and a couple of young fellows arrived with brooms, only to call home asking for shovels and buckets. Joined by Steve, one of the elders in the church, they had me climb the rock staircase that led to the second floor from the outside. The sight was staggering. Huge boulders were piled behind the house to the roof. We could not see the mountain in the dark, but it was clear that something horrific had occurred for which I had no frame of reference.

More friends from church arrived. They all insisted I go elsewhere that night while Peter was returning. I was in shock. I was not yet ready to grasp the reality. My world had just tumbled down, and we were going to face some major hurdles to rebuild our lives. I couldn't know then that an event of that magnitude does not just sweep away; it reveals what you have not yet accomplished and what is not working. It makes you question everything you have created and gives you a second chance to redesign anew.

I had no idea of the challenges ahead of us. It was only six months later, looking at the survivors of Hurricane Katrina, that I wept for them because I knew what they would be facing, how it wouldn't go away overnight, and in fact, their rebuilding would extend into all areas of their lives—physical, emotional, mental, and spiritual. If they embraced the change, they were on the brink of possibility. If they resisted, it would be painful.

Looking back, the landslide was an "*aha*" moment, what some people would call my bottom, as well as the beginning of my conscious pursuit of the process of deliberate creation. This was the most catastrophic event of my life, and yet I learned that we can not only survive but attain something even better. In my case, I gained a new awareness of the creative process and gave myself permission not only to consciously explore it for my own benefit but also to see how I could share this knowledge with others. So many people do not realize that they have the power to create their dreams. They say they want to make a change, but fail to follow through in their actions—and that makes all the difference.

The first eighteen months after the landslide were about survival and being made whole after significant loss. The next two years were about adjusting and regaining our equilibrium in new circumstances. Recovery takes time, willingness, a pinch of courage, the cultivation of a good attitude, and a large dose of faith. We can learn from catastrophe by embracing this process that "works if you work it."

What began as observation and association immediately after the landslide led to an ongoing course of study, first with Fawn Christianson of Sharon Wilson's Coaching from Spirit program to become an "Empowered Spiritual Life Coach." After that, I was drawn to focus on success principles as I studied with Bob Proctor to become a LifeSuccess Consultant. Bob encourages his students to write as a means to reach out to others. Little did I know where this would take me.

I immersed myself into living both the principles and the activities in order to see results. I became aware that success is a process lived on a daily basis through our choices. Success is a continual act of deciding to take actions that move you toward the creation of what you desire. It is a progressive realization through the power of our minds to attain our highest purpose, the worthy ideal that inspires our daily activities over an extended period of time. It fills us with enthusiasm. I came to see that the word *success* is synonymous with the creation of that which did not exist in our lives before we focused on what it would take to do, be, or have it.

The overarching purpose that inspires us may express itself as multiple visions and desires that lead us down a variety of paths. Depending on our dominant thoughts, our paths may change, causing us to grow in several directions. Until we become consciously aware of our thinking, we may even move away from our ideal vision. Fortunately, we are all equipped with an inner gyroscope to bring us back on track if we take the time to evaluate where we are on the journey. We see clues around us in our results.

The key is to focus on the one thing that inspires us within the context of all areas of our lives. Each aspect serves to help our outer environment, inner knowledge, and self-image blend to become the energy vibration that matches our larger dreams. Each vision asks us to achieve a series of goals that are the next logical steps required to move forward in an orderly way.

At times, it felt as if I were lost in a maze of choices. Yet my inner sense of direction would turn back upon itself to bring me new and even better options than I had imagined. I explored the basics of a creative process that yielded what I call "miraculous" solutions in my personal and professional life. This same creative process has made a difference in the lives of countless others who have studied as I have done.

This process, within the context of my experience, is what I wish to share with you, knowing that my life is still a work in progress. It is my earnest desire that the creative success principles may serve to guide you as you define the essence of your dreams and deliberately set out to create and achieve them. They have proved most helpful to me in smoothing the emotional roller coaster that previously plagued me, providing focus, serenity, and strength with which to face life's challenges.

Thank you for choosing me as a traveling companion on this ever-expanding journey. There is a process that helps us choose rainbows over ruins as we create something even better.

S.

Acknowledgments

To colleagues who supported, coached, and cheered me on: Sondra Briggs, Genevieve Gerard, Rev. Barbara Marie Babish, Kathleen Maxwell, and my Coaching From Spirit and LifeSuccess Consultant classmates;

To teachers and mentors who have shared their wealth of knowledge and experience to enhance my own, and reflected back loving support to me when I needed it most: Fawn Christianson, Noah St. John, Marilyn Jenett, Greg Reid, Ted McGrath, and Bob Proctor;

To authors and public speakers whose words have transcended physical interaction to guide my thoughts: Dr. David Hawkins, Dr. Wayne Dyer, Esther and Jerry Hicks, Peggy McColl, Jim Rohn, and Jeff Olson;

To fellow workers who have contributed to my understanding of the creative process as we live it daily; to the staff who have listened to an inspiration, formatted manuscripts, participated in the process of creating a vision board, and volunteered to help create even more;

To friends, family, and those on social media and in other support groups who observed and accompanied me on my journey, sometimes challenging, sometimes accepting, and ultimately grounding me: Amy, Tom and Charlie, Sally Meersman, Susan Scudder, and the Shadow Hills Church community;

To mentees, mastermind groups, and network marketing team members who have allowed me to share the creative process with them;

To all those who are taking up their own creative journey to express the one thing that inspires them to grow, expand, and create something new; and

To those who consciously step out to resolve conflicts and contrasts through the creative process.

CHAPTER 1

BEFORE THE FALL

Most of us go through life without any conscious understanding of a success process. We move from one experience to another without applying any thought to why or what we are doing. We accept our current situations, comfortable when we have food, water, a bed, and a roof over our heads. We become aware that employment and relationships are keys to maintaining these basics, as well as obtaining more, even if we do not always learn how to do it well. Our environment serves to build us up or knock us down, and we roll with it.

A smaller number become proactive, observing ways that their lives could be better, and they pursue those things that appear to lead to those improvements. Without any awareness of a process, they do well. Perhaps they have better educations, families, communities, coaches, or role models. Whatever the reason, they achieve their goals. Success coach Bob Proctor calls them "unconscious competents." This is where my husband, Peter, and I found ourselves when we first met on our daily commute from New Jersey to New York City.

Peter's parents were solid working-class people who imposed strict rules. The male role models around him—father, uncles, neighbors—had been locked in the same jobs for forty years, doing their work the same way, even when they could have created something better. He chafed against their restraints and enlisted in the air force as soon as it was possible. For years, his method of making life decisions was about discovering what he did not want. It was a process of elimination. He was trained in electronics but had no interest in pursuing it as a career. He was transferred to a cold climate and figured out what he needed to do to get assigned to a warmer location. His routine was simple. He worked his job, took extension courses, collected records and comics, and watched Western television shows.

Opportunities evolved. An avid collector, Peter regularly called into a local radio station with the titles of songs they were playing. Eventually, the radio hosts asked him if he had ever thought of being a disc jockey. He barely paused before saying yes. They helped him get his third- class FCC license, but he was still in the service and was transferred away. On that new base, he caught the eye of a lieutenant in charge of Project Transition, a new program to help servicemen transition to civilian life. The officer arranged for Peter to begin working with a local radio station. He enjoyed it but noticed that others around him were better off than he was. They had fancy cars, while he drove a Corvair. They suggested he get a liberal arts degree so that he could talk about anything. So he enrolled at a community college as a speech major. That instructor asked him to be in a play. He loved it. He loved the recognition, the applause, and the variety.

He continued his education, pursuing a BA, theater major, radio TV minor. Peter produced an award-winning documentary that caught the eye of Channel 52, a public TV station in Trenton, New Jersey. He began to work for them two days a week. The opportunity held a great deal of promise; however, when he was offered a full-time position, he turned it down. Instead, he began commuting to New York City to study with Sonia Moore, whose book was one of the textbooks in the theater department, and obtained an MA in conjunction with those studies. There, fellow student Barra N. encouraged Peter to define his own pigeonhole, rather than allowing the entertainment industry to define it for him. He took her words to heart and began to seriously study the American West and acquire items he liked. He had a car, a cabin in northern New Jersey, and a girlfriend, along with all those comics, records, and interests in Western cowboy stuff. Then his cabin was destroyed by fire.

I grew up just a few miles from Peter, but we had never met. My father had pursued his doctorate in psychology and was dean at Rutgers University when my mom became pregnant with me. A social worker, she would later become a director at the American Red Cross. But in a classic case of bad timing, Dad had just left Rutgers to take a good position in Ohio when it became clear that Mom could not travel. It was a hard time. He sold hotdogs off a cart to make ends meet until he could find a new job as a guidance counselor in Freehold, New Jersey. He wanted a better life for his small family and a nicer home. Since his salary was modest and therapy was not well accepted or popular yet, he found additional work in the evenings as a life insurance salesman. Eventually, we moved to the nicer home, complete with a small office, where he could engage in private career counseling while supporting us through insurance sales. Dad was pretty good at sales. His office walls were plastered with million-dollar roundtable certificates. I got to see firsthand how counseling could help people and enjoyed working with my dad whenever he would give me the opportunity to score the Kuder Preference Tests that helped him guide people in their choices. This feeling stayed with me over the years, as I could see people were happier when they were doing what they loved. You could say this was my introduction to the deliberate creation process.

Mom and Dad were active in community service organizations. They valued service as an important aspect of family life. Our home was filled with important people in town, all dedicated to public service. Unfortunately, there was a dark side to this social activity. Both my parents became heavy drinkers. It was called social drinking in those days. Everyone drank. It was part of the social fabric, but my mom gradually was more seriously affected. She became a "functional" alcoholic, meaning that she worked her job by day and came home to drink herself into a blackout before bed. I was terrified by the change in my father when he would come home from the Elks Club, easily angered, barely able to navigate the stairs to the upstairs bedrooms. As a teenager, it was hard to keep the family secrets. I was extremely angry. I wanted to hurt them in some way. But they were also good people, and I loved them.

Mom was very concerned with social appearances. She was active in the Presbyterian Church, not for the opportunities of faith and service but because it was the place where one could make the best connections.

When I was twelve, she insisted that I take my confirmation, threatening to prevent social interactions if I refused. I confirmed; however, I was already seeking a truth that was inherent in all faiths, and her heavy- handed threat caused a rift in our relationship that lasted for decades. I pursued a college-prep curriculum, filled with activities in music, dance, theater, and the honor society, as well as church programs, where I met my first husband. Heading off to college, I wanted to pursue music, dance, and theater; however, once again, my parents imposed their point of view, insisting that I study something that could provide a more reliable income. I studied some psychology, but my BA degree was in English education, with a minor in music. As a college student, I plotted out the exact path of my life—the MRS that we joked about in those days. My high school sweetheart and I married during our senior year of college and started our family. The whole family was thrilled when daughter Amy arrived.

Unfortunately, I wasn't very good at living the life of a stay-at-home mom. The question that loomed in my mind was, "Is this all there is?" The contrast I felt between "something more" and my experience was crushing. To alleviate this distress, my father suggested we buy a small bookstore for my mother-in-law, Marty, and me to manage. What a radical idea that was! There was no women's liberation in those days, and the banks would not lend us money without the men in our lives cosigning the note. So two dads and my husband, an insurance claims adjustor, signed for us, and Marty and I spent the next few years working in the bookstore together. We had a great time running the Book Fair, specializing in children's books, in spite of the fact that I was struggling with the emotional upheavals that accompany a failing marriage. We split the workload in what we now call job sharing.

That's when I found television psychologist Dr. Joyce Brothers's book *The Brothers System for Liberated Love and Marriage*. Working with the exercises in her book, I had my second experience with the deliberate creation process.

Over the space of a few weeks, I was to (a) list six things I needed in order to feel the positive feelings I wanted, for example, to be happy, more fulfilled, hopeful, and so on; (b) brainstorm about all the reasons why I could not have these things; (c) brainstorm about all the ways I could overcome those reasons; and then (d) pick one, just one, action I could take from all those potential solutions. Dr. Brothers said that it would be like starting a snowball rolling downhill. It would set things in motion to bring me what I wanted.

It is one thing to want something. It is another to decide to take a single action that will move you forward. One of my favorite quotes is attributed to the philosopher Goethe, saying that once you are clear on your desire, the universe will work day and night to attract it into your life. Making the choice of a single action unleashes the power of the universe around your intentions. I worked the exercises. They provided an awareness of what I needed to do in order to make changes in my life. Our tiny little bookstore, nestled between an auto-parts store and a barbershop, barely made enough to pay the bills, let alone salaries. The most important result I could get was to find a full-time job that paid. Marty and I sold the bookstore. Amy's dad enrolled in law school. Our little family of three found a small apartment near the Jersey shore so we could stop living with my parents, and I went to work. Law school can be a challenging time for marriages. It certainly was for us. Joy drained out of our relationship over the three years of study, and shortly after he passed the bar exam, we divorced.

At that point, I wanted to perform. I enrolled in a school of commercial acting in New York City, where the textbook seemed an unlikely choice for those of us involved in the craft of acting. It was Napoleon Hill's *The Master Key to Riches,* and yet a third time, I was exposed to success principles that fuel the deliberate creation process. I moved on to work auditing for a major entertainment studio in the city by day and studying acting in the evening. Each night I would catch the last bus home to New Jersey. Unbeknown to me, another actor rode that same bus every night, and after some time, Earl, the bus driver, introduced us. It turned out to be my future husband, Peter.

Both of us had been going through some personal traumas. Even at five, my daughter, Amy, knew that she did not want to live in

Manhattan. Now a young divorcee, I was at a loss to provide a good income, commute, and keep her safe. Eventually, she moved in with her dad. With the loss of his cabin, Peter was every bit the struggling actor. It took years for our relationship to get serious, but we became great friends. I was able to share what I was learning about the power of positive thinking from Napoleon Hill, and it was making a huge difference in the attitude we each brought to our careers and personal lives. Both of us were moving toward our goals in the entertainment industry and sharing our dreams about the future.

Hill began his work when industrialist Andrew Carnegie suggested he study the most successful people in the world to find out what they had in common. Hill spent over twenty years interviewing five hundred people and finally published the business bestseller *Think and Grow Rich*. At first, Peter and I were most influenced by Hill's emphasis on positive thinking, although his writings were far more expansive than that. Hill's philosophy permeated our lives, consciously and unconsciously. I want to emphasize the word *unconsciously* because in retrospect I realize that Peter and I accomplished quite a bit of dreaming and creative imagining without really knowing that these were among the components of inner work that occur before we can move an idea from a possibility to a tangible reality.

One of our hobbies was to write stories and movie plots, as well as ponder where we wanted to go in our careers and how we might accomplish our goals. We wrote one script in particular, *Caravan West*, which was the story of a young couple chasing a truck across country to rescue a horse that had been stolen from an auction. It was inspired by the buyers from the meat-packing companies that frequented the horse auctions we visited weekly. We fantasized about making that trip ourselves and filming it documentary style as we traveled from New York to California. And in time, we decided to make that trip—not with the camera but with the horses. This would have been a no-brainer now in the day of camcorders, but no one I knew even owned a VHS player in 1980. Little did we know that this adventure would become far more than a journey of only a few months.

The trip was challenging. We took over two months to get across the country with our little caravan, which included a pickup truck, car, and Winnebago hauling a horse trailer. Wayne, the eighteen-year-old nephew of a family friend, shared the driving, looking forward to seeing his brother on the West Coast. So after weeks on the road, when we arrived in San Diego County on Christmas Eve, the last thing he wanted was to spend one more night in that camper. He had his brother pick him up, leaving us with three vehicles and only two drivers, parked on the service road next to a freeway.

A major holiday is not the time to arrive unplanned in an unknown city looking for a stable to house your horses. There was no room at the inn anywhere in Ramona, California, the city where we had landed. We had more challenges to come. Unbeknown to us, Wayne had washed his laundry in our cooler, using the last of our drinking water. We slept that night with one eye open to monitor the horses, which were hobbled beside us. As Christmas morning dawned, we made our way to a baseball field, where we could let the horses out in a contained environment. As we were also at the end of our food supplies, Peter went to find water and breakfast for us. I waited, trying to create a Christmas celebration.

I did not have much to work with—no Christmas tree, not much in the way of presents, barely any food, and no place to go or way to go there for the moment. What we did have was a great deal of anxiety in an unfamiliar environment. The inspiration that came to me was to create a Christmas tree out of wrapping paper—a brown roll and one more festive. The tree itself was made out of the brown paper. And it was decorated with balls of the colored gift wrap. On each of the balls, I wrote either what we had to be grateful for, what we had accomplished to get where we were, or a dream we still wanted to see happen.

By the time Peter returned with a pound of bacon, a dozen eggs, a loaf of bread, and a bottle of wine, we had the makings of a lovely little holiday breakfast. However, no sooner had we turned on the stove to cook, than the Winnebago ran out of propane. Laughing at the latest chain of events, we decided to make the best of the situation, celebrating our holiday with the only gifts we had thought to purchase coming across country and laughing how one day this would all be a wonderful memory.

And that's when what we call our "gift of the magi" miracle occurred. Two men from the neighborhood, out riding their horses, came upon us. They invited us back to their home to celebrate the holiday with them and their families. Cesar and Rosa offered us stable space for the horses and dogs. They gave us tours of Tijuana, the tourist city just over the border in Mexico. The friendships we made that holiday have stayed with us all these years, no matter how much time and space have intervened. We finally arrived in Los Angeles a few weeks later, with our last three hundred dollars, located a campground to make our home, and began to build what turned out to be our new life in California. We had a vision of our acting careers at that point, but much to accomplish to get there. We made friends with other actors, one of whom invited me to swing on a trapeze in someone's backyard. It was quite something to learn to fly a trapeze!

First, I had to climb up a twenty-foot rope ladder, which was exhausting all by itself. Then I stood on a platform, and the instructor placed the trapeze bar in my hands.

"Just step off the platform while hanging onto the bar," she said. But I couldn't do it.

"Relax," she said.

I could not make my muscles respond. I was frozen. It was as if my feet were welded to the platform. I couldn't get my body to jump, step, or any word you can use to describe how to accomplish the goal. I couldn't understand what was stopping me. I couldn't translate any of the trainer's suggestions into what I had to do to let go and swing.

Other flyers would step up to the edge of the platform and take off easily. They talked to me, explaining what to do. It seemed like forever before I finally stepped into it. As I surrendered to the experience and "flew"—swinging back and forth, my hands had a death grip on the bar even as I experienced the incredible sensation of swinging on a trapeze. How exhilarating it was! After a few swings, they told me to let go and drop into the net. Amazingly, I even climbed back up and did it a second time. Do I know what made the difference? I believe that ultimately it was seeing that other people could swing without harm.

While I stood on that platform, other people were doing what I was being asked to do, building up a powerful image that I could grab onto and hold viscerally, when words were not enough. The images provided positive reinforcement that flying was possible whenever I was ready. I was surrounded by an image of the joyful experience of flying.

Over the next few years, we would earn our livelihoods with day jobs. I worked with lawyers and moved into business affairs and international sales with production companies. My career vision slowly shifted from the smaller professional roles I was able to secure here and there toward the producing team, where I found I could contribute more to the overall creative product.

Peter found steady work entertaining at children's parties and making appearances for Marvel Comics. We were busy making friends, getting agents and managers, participating in celebrity charity events, and otherwise doing whatever we perceived would help us to move to the next level. Four years later, we had made enough progress to get married and purchase a home.

Since this was Peter's first wedding, we designed it to meet his needs as well as my own. I wore a beige lace dress he had innocently picked out for me at a swap meet. We chose an older ring found in a pawnshop. Our housemate, Ruth K., crafted a hat with lace veils, and I borrowed a belt to wear with the dress. Amy flew in from New Jersey, and Pat M. joined us from northern California to be in the wedding party. It was a marvelous girls' night when we made our own bouquets for the ceremony.

Meanwhile, Peter was adding his own special touches. All of his friends were asked to attend in classic Old West frock coats. He and his best man, Joe D., arrived on horseback. When the ceremony was complete, Peter captured me according to ancient traditions, placing me on horseback to ride around the area for a few minutes. It was a glorious day, surrounded by good friends and western trappings.

Unified by this event, our vision expanded. We wanted to get a larger ranch for ourselves and the animals. Peter was acting, but also indulging his passion for the Old West to an ever greater extent, performing in Wild West shows and collecting authentic items from life during the nineteenth century. When not working, my spiritual studies led me to psychosynthesis, a transpersonal psychology developed by Italian psychiatrist Dr. Roberto Assagioli.

A colleague of Freud and Jung, Assagioli collaborated with Abraham Maslow. Maslow's booklet *The Creative Attitude* was published by the Psychosynthesis Research Foundation in 1963. In a photographic book compiled after Assagioli's death, an unattributed, undated article credited to *New Yorker Magazine* quotes a "Murphy" saying that what "Abe Maslow called self-actualization... Assagioli called psychosynthesis." What they shared in common was the idea that "there is a natural tendency toward evolution, toward unfoldment, that pervades the universe as well as the human sphere, and that our job now is to get behind that and make it conscious."

I can still remember my first class, in which Assagioli's map of consciousness was explained to me. It looked just like an egg that was divided in three parts, containing the personal "I" surrounded by the conscious mind. The subconscious or lower unconscious was below the conscious mind, and a superconscious layer was above it. Surrounding this view of personal consciousness was a collective consciousness, a higher power. We find our transpersonal, or higher, self at the point where superconscious and the collective unconscious meet.

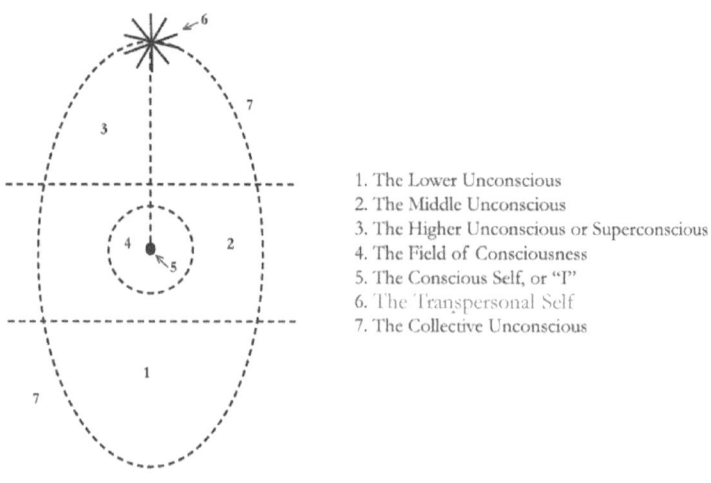

1. The Lower Unconscious
2. The Middle Unconscious
3. The Higher Unconscious or Superconscious
4. The Field of Consciousness
5. The Conscious Self, or "I"
6. The Transpersonal Self
7. The Collective Unconscious

Assagioli's Map of Consciousness

Since Assagioli and Maslow felt our "job" was to make the process of evolution conscious, we were asked to participate in an exercise that gave me a conscious sensation of connecting with my higher self. If you pray or meditate, you are familiar with this inner space. If not, you may find it naturally in quiet contemplation, when alone with nature or sitting by a fire. But you may also be guided to the experience. This happened to me through what is called a dis-identification exercise. It is a process of withdrawing our conscious thinking from the external, physical world to focus on an inner space that remains when there are no other distractions.

The memories of that first guided journey are still with me years later. Our class was gathered on sofas in the late Vivian King's (author of *Being Here When I Need Me)* living room, all sitting comfortably as she had us close our eyes. Vivian always had candles with pleasant aromas to enhance the environment.

As we sat, she had us check in with our physical bodies. "What are you feeling? Can you feel the chair or sofa beneath you? Do you feel any tension? Do you feel any pain? Feel your body. If you feel any discomfort, ask your body to put it aside for the moment. Tuck it into a recess of your mind. It will not be forgotten. You will come back to it. You have a body, but you are not just your body. Your body serves you well. It is an instrument for action, but you are much more than your body."

Next, she had us get in touch with our emotions. "Are you happy, angry, frustrated, sad, afraid, worried, or overwhelmed? Whatever you are feeling, ask that your emotions also recede to a corner of your mind. You will come back for them as well. Your emotions serve you well. They are a barometer for what is happening in your life, for the contrasts that prompt you to seek change. But you are not just your emotions. You are much more than your emotions."

What of our thoughts? "Ask that the continual flow of thoughts yield its place within your mind. You will be back for them. You have thoughts, but you are not just your thoughts. Your thoughts can serve you well in the process of discrimination, but you are much more than your thoughts."

For me, what remained was a gentle, comfortable silence. Here in this space, "you are a centered being of Light, Love and Power." This was my first conscious experience of what is called by many names—my higher self, subconscious, supraconscious, transpersonal self—nonlinear, nonverbal, peaceful, serene, and powerful. I centered in this space, opening to something deeper from within. I ceased the effort to control the outcome and yielded. Whatever I dreamed of accomplishing, something greater than my conscious self would be my greatest ally and resource.

Over three years, I earned certificates as a trainer in psychosynthesis. During that time, I was introduced to various schools of thought, introductory concepts of quantum physics, and possibilities that were outside my day-to-day experiences, but I was not interested in becoming a therapist. Continuing my spiritual studies and talking with others about pursuing their dreams was my avocation.

I was actively engaged in making and marketing television films and series. Peter's successes as an actor were growing. Writers and directors began to be part of our social circle. He had his first costarring roles in *Death Wish IV* and starred in a little-known feature called *Black Snow.* He began to rent a few items to films, even starting his business under the name Caravan West Productions. And when we stopped to dream together, we talked about producing movies on a big ranch.

So how did I think we could get to make movies? I thought it would make sense to get an MBA and use what I learned to become very good at deal making. Indulging an entrepreneurial bent, I wrote a business plan for a business incubator, Film Offices Plus. Over the next five years, I pursued my degree at Woodbury University in Burbank. In the end, I spent far less time on deals and more on management. I jumped on an opportunity to move to a senior-level management position in postproduction for what turned out to be a three-year interlude.

At some point, I sought out the services of Bennett Dolan, a career counselor, to help me clarify the direction I wanted to take. My objective was to find or create a position that could integrate my skills with my dreams and values. Much as the earlier Dr. Brothers's exercises helped me choose a single action to take, Ben helped me narrow the field of possibilities so that I could focus. Once again, it started with a list—the top twelve items that meant the most to me. My list was actually longer than that and very diverse. I wanted to write; work for a broadcaster; house manage a theater; work in sales; produce; turn Caravan West into a real business; work for an entertainment lawyer, an Internet company, an NPO, a completion bond company; start a business incubator; work in real estate, accounting, financial investing, business management; be a buyer, a financial analyst; manage a foundation; work for a guild; or teach. It was no wonder that I was confused.

The fun and challenging part was to narrow the list down. I played with the list on yellow-lined notebooks, school notebooks, and steno pads until I had a list of twelve, with a sentence written about each one. For another pass, I had to cut the list in half, writing a paragraph about six items and then a full page on three. I found I could retain qualities of an idea by combining it with others, rather than eliminating it. Ultimately, I had to choose one thing that brought me the most joy as I played with the idea of creating it.

Even I was a little surprised as I pulled out my old notes from this exercise that I came very close to describing what I am doing now as line producer for a daily television series for a broadcaster with similar values. I work with house managers, lawyers, accountants, and ad sales, along with our producers, operations staff, and social media, and strive to maintain a workplace that supports a highly creative environment. But I wasn't close to this when I made that list. It would be ten years before I would begin to close in on this position, and by then, I would have added one more item to my wish list after reading Gail Sheehey's book *New Passages*.

Gail's premise was that as we live longer in our society, we will find additional careers to help us live full, rich lives in our senior years. Retirement would take on a new meaning. She invited her readers to define what their "retirement" career would be. In the distant future, I saw myself coordinating or running a space where people could come to search, look at, and explore their dreams. It had no connection with my life at the time, and for fifteen years, I joked about retiring to direct a retreat center or business incubator. It seemed beyond the realm of possibility. What credentials did I have? Who would listen to me? I worked in television. I believed I would have to redefine myself to accomplish this idea.

So Peter and I kept building our careers. *Tombstone* moved him to a new level, but when we penned his first book based on his work on the film, it sat on the shelf for years. Caravan West started to grow. We discovered he had a talent for this, and we focused more on his business. He had a serious horse wreck just before starting to shoot our first filmshort, but he bounced back and we produced a stage play, *Cody, An Evening with Buffalo Bill,* and then filmed it.

After completing my MBA, I was back in production, working my way up the ranks. I was active in the Producers Guild of America, producing monthly seminars for the benefit of our membership. All of that seemed good. However, I was also developing the habit of having a couple of glasses of wine or brandy or bourbon when I came home at night, and it was having its effect on me. I did not want to admit it, but I had an internal feeling that something was wrong and at some point I was going to have to face it.

When that landslide hit in 2005, we were aware that we had outgrown our home. We had a strong idea of what we would like someday; however, we had not been able to see how we would be able to make it happen. We did not believe it was in the realm of possibility. What we did not realize was that we were using language repeatedly that, coupled with our sense of humor, created an environment ripe for something to shift toward the creation of something new. And shift it did.

CHAPTER 2

ESCAPE, RESCUE, AND RECOVERY

I'd like to be able to say that I moved right into thoughts of how I would recreate my world, setting out a purpose and plan that expressed what I wanted, in those first moments and days after arriving at the scene of the slide, but I didn't. I prefer to think that even the most optimistic people have to travel through escape, rescue, and recovery before they can contemplate the future again—because that is what I did. Looking back, I tend to think that there is some hint in the items we decide to take with us in that moment, revealing what will help us begin the rebuilding process.

All of my desires collapsed to the lowest point of stability, concerns for physical health and safety. Only hours earlier, I had been pondering what we would want to do next as new opportunities emerged. In the aftermath, I was walking and talking with the small band of folks who came to support me that night. I was making instantaneous decisions that came more from instinct than any logical reasoning. I was in shock. Strictly in survival mode, I focused in the immediate moment, right where we were.

Having determined that our menagerie was not in imminent danger, those who came from the church to help were uncomfortable with me staying in the house by myself until Peter's return. Judyth offered a spot on the sofa at her home, which I accepted. I took a couple of boxes of Peter's newly released book, my computer with family photos, a Remington bronze, a small overnight bag, some valuable papers, and perhaps most critically, a couple of books that I would find useful over the next months, including Wayne Dyer's *There Is a Spiritual Solution to Every Problem*.

Peter arrived home at 2:00 a.m. and would not leave the house, feeling the need to protect his belongings. All the utilities still worked, so Peter made sure the wires to the TV were high and dry and immediately turned on the television set. On the other hand, when I returned, I was too frightened to even sit down in the house.

Later, each person who came to help or see the damage had to come to terms with what he or she found. The entire floor was covered in mud, but people would wipe their feet on the mat outside and step into the muddy room. Peter's friend Larry observed the leak overhead in the living room ceiling and asked me to get a pot to catch the water that was dripping onto the already muddy floor. For me, it had a touch of black humor that made no sense. We all fell back on our habits, even when strangely absurd, in the face of such destruction.

By dawn, the damage outside the house was evident. Two swaths of soil above the house had let go. On one side, the rocks and muddy earth had crashed against the house, piling up to the roof, through the upstairs windows, across the hall, and into the bathroom. Bookshelves were covered in mud. The water had traveled down the stairs, pouring through the balustrade into the living room, where the items closest to the staircase had been damaged. Carpeting was soaked in muddy water, and windows had been broken. More water hit the opposing wall and turned in the other direction, flowing across the dining room and down a flight of stairs to a small basement area, pulling down the ceiling tiles and soaking the wallboard. This was a hat room, lined with Stetson hats now coated with mud and other household construction materials. The second swath of mud had crashed into the laundry room area, creating a crack through which water would flow with each passing rainstorm. The flowing earth had filled the patio with approximately five to six feet of mud, completely burying a staircase to the back kitchen door. There was no way to open that door. We could not see that the spigot in that area had been damaged, allowing a small amount of water to continuously leak from the pipe. All the larger set dressing that Peter stored outside on the patio was buried and destroyed. Mud flowed across the patio into the garage and around the front corner of the house. When I went up and down stairs, I had a sense that they were "off." It was not something discernible to the eye for months, at which point I finally saw that a major bearing beam had shifted and was gradually pushing its way through the plaster walls.

The fire department arrived the next morning to "red tag" the house. A term used commonly in California during disasters, red tag is the nickname for the red condemnation sign they use. Due to the nature of Western props, Peter would not leave them unlocked inside an empty house so the firemen helped him move a variety of items out. The insurance adjuster came by to inform us that there was no insurance on the house or its contents. Landslides and mudslides had proven so expensive that all insurers had stopped covering them.

But there were bright spots too. The phone rang in the house a couple of days after the slide. It was a producer looking for Peter's services. We had lost a significant amount of set dressing and props, but the Buckaroos, mounted and costumed background players who work with Peter, and the horses could still work; a portion of the wardrobe was above the damage; and items that were in huge trunks were still usable. We made a decision in that moment that I have always felt made the biggest difference in getting us on track quickly. We consciously chose, then and there, to accept the work in spite of the catastrophe around us. We had a long road ahead with no time like the present to start the process. Crying about the past and what had occurred was not going to help. We had to get through what had happened somehow. It was right in front of us, and working would put us in the right frame of mind.

The relationships I had built within my church community proved invaluable. The Shadow Hills Church, located in the eastern valley, is in an area of Los Angeles that still keeps horses. It is a small church with a country feeling. Its congregation is made up of hospitable people who truly care for one another, and in our time of need, they cared for us. Jim and Deidre put us up in their home for six weeks until we could find a rental that would take us and our menagerie. Derek and Sharon allowed us to keep our horses in the backyard stables of an empty house they owned. Bird and cat found a home with Laura and Andy. The fencing had been destroyed, so the dogs could not be kept on the property safely until things settled down. We found a kennel down the street, and our favorite veterinarian, Dr. Sahi, even offered to keep his favorite of our dogs at his office.

In spite of the ongoing danger at the house, everyone turned out to help us empty the badly damaged rooms and get items into trucks. The men arranged a car shuttle to move our belongings into storage units. The women helped us pack the glasses and dishware. Some of the simplest gifts were also the most meaningful. Laura brought me clean, dry socks and Mary Ann thought I could use industrial-style boots because it continued to rain and we were working day in and day out in the mud. Every new deluge flooded the floors of the house, so nothing ever dried out.

What happened over the next few weeks was surreal. There was no readily accessible manual for assistance, nor did I have the time or ability to research the subject. We didn't know what was next or what our options were. We had to learn to take each day a day at a time, for each day would bring some new crisis to solve. We would confront the situation, ask questions, and seek out the answers. I was becoming physically ill from the stress, because the answers were not easy to come by and the potential headaches were huge.

Where would we find immediate shelter? Places like the Red Cross are set up to serve masses of people at one time. They were not really ready to assist a single family with a menagerie.

What were the financial impacts? Not only was there no insurance money coming to us, but we would also have to pay both our mortgage and the homeowners insurance even though no one could live on the property. We were going to have to find new housing and continue to pay for the old.

Was there any type of government assistance? This looked to be a never-ending nightmare. Again, most of the disaster relief programs were set up to handle mass catastrophes, not individual occurrences.

There were no government programs available to us. In fact, we found ourselves suddenly facing government fines for having zoning violations where the rocks had fallen. As owners, we had to move the rocks. I called the city to find out just how to do that. They told me to call a geologist. I pulled out the yellow pages and started calling. Who knew how many different specialists existed? I could not find the right job title or the person who could direct me to the right specialist. The threat from the government, coupled with trying to identify the "soil" geologist who could tell us what needed to be done, created a gnawing pit in my stomach. It felt like a catch-22. With huge boulders stacked perilously behind the house, we could not remove them without guidance, and unless we found someone who could provide that expertise to do it, we would be penalized.

It was at this point that we began to contemplate the next steps in our survival and rebuilding. Napoleon Hill wrote in *The Law of Success* that anything is possible if you have a purpose and a plan enhanced by continuous, conscious concentration on those ideas. We weren't thinking of success principles, but we seemed to intuitively apply the concept. It became abundantly clear that our immediate goal was to find a new home for our family, which had been spread out throughout the city. This was not a casual desire. We were intensely focused on it. We focused *all* our attention on it.

My morning routine had been to read inspirational passages and meditate daily. In my new, temporary living arrangement, I continued the practice, reading from the Wayne Dyer book I had taken with me. During this time period, it felt as if small miracles, like "God shots" or "God winks," were happening. Our hostess had a colleague whose uncle was an expert witness in geology trials. He recommended several attorneys specializing in landslide law. One of those attorneys was willing to take our case on contingency. He told us to get on with our lives, as it would take a couple of years to work through the situation. He took on all the headaches connected with the city, which was a huge relief. I was inspired to search for a home to rent, and one of the first realtors I called had a house that had just been listed. It hadn't even been in the papers yet. The place was perfect. The owners welcomed our full family, and it was near the church. Serendipity.

As this was playing out, I was aware of a sensation that a power greater than myself was guiding me, literally holding my hand through this entire crisis. Before you shake your head and put down this book, you might want to consider that today's quantum physicists describe something they call the zero-point field, because at some infinitesimal level, some sort of force appears to be present. "At a deep and fundamental level, the 'separate' parts of the universe are connected in an intimate and immediate way" (*The Dancing Wu Li Masters,* by Gary Zukav, p. 282). It's not energy, nor is it empty space. Metaphorically, it appears to be a "sea" of pure consciousness (business coach and success speaker John Assaraf and Murray Smith, *The Answer,* p. 15) made up of surrounding waves of possibility.

Assaraf and Smith describe consciousness as "what the universe is made of; matter and energy are just two of the forms that consciousness takes." Dr. Amit Goswami (author, *God Is Not Dead*) bears this out. Matter and energy are just two of the multiple "domains of quantum possibilities of consciousness" (*God Is Not Dead,* p. 25). As Goswami describes it, more exist outside time and space as waves of possibility. It is all one unity until a choice is made, via consciousness, to look at a single possibility, at which point it "collapses" into the certainty of a particle. This is the basis of the understanding that thought creates everything. Energy follows thought.

I bring this up so that you may explore the science of these ideas if you are so inclined, as there is empirical evidence that energy outside the space-time continuum (unseen, nonphysical) can affect us. Pure consciousness affects matter through "downward causation." No energy is exchanged; instead, this effect is accomplished by "nonlocality," "discontinuity," and "tangled hierarchy." Goswami labels these as "quantum signals of the divine." Most people cannot verify their experience of this through scientific experiments. Instead, they rely as I did on my impression of being led by the hand in a comforting way.

I was also aware that the community of the church was a key to my survival. The people I expected to help were not the ones who did.

My coworkers barely skipped a beat in their workday. That was quite an eye-opener. Those of us in the entertainment industry often speak of sacrificing our personal lives to meet production demands. There is no malice involved; people are just overwhelmed. However, recognizing how that affects others at a moment of need, it began to have a profound impact on my life.

We found a rental house in Shadow Hills. Having found it, we turned our attention to doing whatever we needed to do to solve our financial situation. But now, our goal had expanded. The house was lovely; however, the one thing we wanted was to be in our own home again, replacing or repairing the one we had. A good part of our free time over the next year and a half would be doing whatever our attorney requested and talking about the kind of house we would want and where we would like to live. And I would be looking at my life in a new way, asking myself questions about the meaning behind all that had happened and studying something new to me called centered prayer (silent prayer that seeks to minimize conscious thought).

Within six weeks of moving into the house, affectionately called the Pink Palace due to its pink marble floors, both Peter and I sustained injuries. It was the culmination of all the moving we had been doing for weeks. The straw that broke Peter's back was lifting a very lightweight rocking chair. Mine was a gradual weakening of my arm until I could no longer lift a coffeepot. We had never been to a chiropractor before, but in order to recover from these injuries, I would take part in neuro-emotional work, a kinesiology or muscle-testing technique often utilized by chiropractors to access unconscious problems that become physical symptoms.

I found that this work gently revealed old and new emotional wounds that had been exposed after the landslide. Language itself was revealing. Phrases like "my world came tumbling down" convey the image of a great physical event and accompanying emotional trauma. When the experience actually happened to me, I found I needed to understand the meaning in those words, not just in my external world but in my parallel feeling life. I would journal after chiropractic visits. Often, the treatment coupled with writing triggered emotional breakthroughs. One of these was startling, as I explored the complex effect that my parents' drinking had had upon me. I wanted to explore what was available to foster a deeper healing around that issue and immersed myself in a twelve-step program, adhering to guiding principles that outlined a specific course of action. These programs help people overcome a variety of problematic habit patterns. I came to describe them as a classic success system at work.

Over time I would see that support systems echo throughout our communities in a variety of forms: fellowships, networks, and religious organizations among them. Inherent in their structure is the belief that everything in life is impelled to action through an invisible life force, a power greater than anyone or anything. We can consciously align with this force, regularly and systematically, as individuals or within the context of a group, through prayer, meditation, intention, or observation, as part of a process to effect change. In the process, we can establish new habits.

Ironically, it would be five years before I would remember that this was described in that earlier book I had studied on positive thinking, *The Master Key to Riches* by Napoleon Hill. He called this force the Law of Cosmic Habitforce, describing it as "Nature's method of giving fixation to all habits so that they may carry on automatically once they have been set into motion" (*The Master Key to Riches*, p. 144). Hill had been searching for an ingredient missing from his classic *Think and Grow Rich* for fully twenty years after its publication before he realized that people were only randomly applying the sixteen principles in the original book. They needed consistency to become successful. This would come if they developed habits, rhythms, and patterns in their daily lives that echoed the habits of nature itself.

Through my exposure to several groups, I have come to see that there is a deliberate creation process that combines our physical, emotional, mental, and spiritual thoughts and actions in order to lead to the accomplishment or achievement of anything when undertaken by conscious choice. Habitforce is central to maintaining progress, but the most significant action anyone can take to activate this process and get the desired results is to focus on an idea until it takes on a life of its own.

The best place to start is with the questions "What do you want?" and "Why do you want it?" Take the publication of Peter's first book as an example. He wanted to write a book that would explain not only his story of the making of the film *Tombstone* but also the extent of the historical research that went into it. Why? It would answer the myriad number of questions he had received from people who enjoyed the film, and provide him with a means to educate others in the film industry so more authentic projects could get made.

Once we defined what we wanted, we developed a preliminary plan for its achievement through conscious thought. Neither Peter nor I had ever written or published a book, so the plan was pretty sketchy. Remembering back twenty years, it was probably no more than a vague outline of who and what made up the movie that he wanted to discuss. However, it was enough to move to the next step, which was to develop relationships within a community of like-minded people, whose path to create (or survive) helped foster a belief that we could do it too.

In this case, Peter had several close friends who had either written or published their own books and artwork. Among his Buckaroos (the historically accurate background players in *Tombstone*) were the artist Jerry Crandall and his wife. Judy, who had just published her book on cowgirls, connected us with her publisher, who expressed interest in our book and gave us the technical details for how to prepare it for publication. We became a tiny band who set up photographic paper rolls in our backyard to photograph everything seen in the book over the space of a weekend, augmented by an assistant to organize all the resulting images.

The next requirement in the process was that we work with the conscious and nonconscious aspects of our minds to change both physical habits and thought patterns (paradigms) that controlled our lives in order to support new goals and directives. Once we had the photos, Peter and I had to write the book. That required giving up hours of free time for months. Peter documented his research and wrote the chapters by hand. I then input them to the computer, editing and making suggestions. We wrote captions for each photo, conforming them to the publisher's directions for inclusion in the book. Finally, all the pieces were ready for delivery. We shipped the materials to the publisher and sat back to wait for proof copies.

In the simplest understanding of Napoleon Hill's success process, we were to continue to hold the wonderful feelings associated with our vision, but let go of conscious control. The reality is that the book did not come together at that time. The publisher did not want the version we had created after all. We were going to have to hold our vision, manuscript on the shelf, for ten years until another writer, George Layman, asked if we knew anyone who had written a book. *Shoot Magazine* was looking for one. The rest is history. Within the year, the book was a reality, and we were enjoying the results of the natural creative process.

CHAPTER 3

IT ALL BEGINS WITH AN IDEA

The most important takeaway from the story in the previous chapter is that the deliberate creation process begins when you know the one thing you want and place your attention on it for as long as it takes to attain. It is an inner and an outer process that occurs simultaneously in one's thoughts, feelings, and actions.

I've heard that as many as 80,000 thoughts pass through our minds each day. Some are sense-based, meaning that they are things we see, hear, smell, touch, and taste. Many people seem to operate entirely from what is around them in the outer world. But there are other aspects to thinking that we call the intellectual faculties, which are perception, reasoning, memory, will, intuition, and imagination. We experience those aspects, located within our own minds, internally without direct input from our senses.

What matters to each of us individually is that out of the thousands of thoughts we think daily, a few ideas will resonate more strongly with us. We get interested in them. We spend a little more time, contemplate and play, with those few until we experience them as something we desire.

As we continue to devote more energy to the most interesting ideas, we develop what Sharon Wilson, the chief inspiration officer at Coaching from Spirit, calls an "energetic blueprint." It is a helpful tool when we are not consciously aware of a developing vision. Like detectives, we find clues in the thought patterns that desire leaves. For instance, one way we know what we value is by where we spend our money. Where is that recorded? In our checkbook registers. Wilson's empowered spiritual life coaches help their clients see these blueprints by asking questions about their beliefs and patterns. Some of these will serve them well. Others will not. Using their answers, coach and client work together to uncover both passions and problems. These are then translated into a blueprint of the ideas someone would want to amplify, as well as new beliefs that can replace patterns that undermine their largest goals.

If you are not clear on what you want, you are not alone. Only a small percentage of the world's population knows what they want. The rest have a sense, an internal discomfort, that there is something they want to do, be, or have, but they cannot put their finger on it or articulate it. They may be afraid to explore it, to birth it. And yes, some do not believe they deserve the good of it. The result is that they tend to wander around without any focus, often just going through the motions of surviving.

Knowing what you want is a critical component to anyone's success at anything. It's so important that almost every author and teacher in the personal development field speaks about it. And certainly every athletic coach makes it part of his or her coaching discipline. Call it purpose, "the one thing," a "reason for being," your primary goal or objective. Most of the multiple personal-development programs, articles, and books center on helping people identify what they want so that they can focus and apply the other principles that become the process that makes things happen.

Why is this so important? Going back to quantum physics, we are surrounded by infinite waves of possibility. For anything to happen, we have to focus on one of those possibilities, whether it's as simple as the kind of coffee we drink or as complex as a life's work. We go through this process continuously in a variety of tasks.

With an idea in mind, we send out thought streams that resonate with similar elements in our environment. I may have sat in the same room for years, but am suddenly aware of things around me that relate to a new idea. When I am writing, certain books in my office library seem to pop off the shelves, or I may be inspired to pick up a pen or notepad only to have the book that contains just what I need appear next to my hand.

When you identify what you want, ideas that are perfect solutions pop into your mind. Maxwell Maltz (author, *Psycho-Cybernetics*) describes this sudden awareness as a "servomechanism" that is built into our physical operation to help us survive. It is an extremely subtle, self-correcting mechanism, much like a gyroscope, that shows us when we have wandered off the course we set. The more detail we can supply the system about why we have set our sail one way, the less time we spend wandering off in the wrong direction and the less time is required for course corrections. (As an aside, we still spend far more time off course that anyone realizes.) So when we have identified a strong call toward something (even if vague), it becomes our job to identify it, decide that we are going to explore it, pay attention to the clues that begin to come to us, and take action.

But how do we begin? It may sound simplistic, but it can be as easy as making lists and asking questions. Do you want a car? What kind of a car? Do you need to pay for the car? What do you want to do in order to get the money? Why do you want the car? Where do you want to go in the car? What do you want to do with the car? There are no rules or limits. We begin by identifying a slight recognized contrast between where we are and what we want, an urge to take action or a strong purpose, vision, or goal that dominates our thinking.

It's easy to jot down a list of simple, tangible ideas no matter where we are. However, when more complicated desires require us to tap into waves of possibility, it's a good idea to seek a quiet time and place. Sacred spaces, beautiful views, gardens, beaches, and parks provide an environment for reflection that aligns with our higher self. For myself, I find mountains inspirational, helping me to expand my thoughts.

Meditation and the dis-identification exercise I learned in psychosynthesis also help us gain a purposeful focus, providing access to insights from the surrounding quantum consciousness. Centered prayer would be another powerful technique used to minimize the mind's conscious activity in order to open to pure consciousness. The method is simple: Think of one word of one or two syllables that you like (peace, love, father, mother, and grace are examples) and keep thinking that word in whatever form it takes. When you become aware of some other thought pulling you away, return to the word chosen. It can be any perception that floats across the inner screen of your mind. You may be intrigued and want to explore such distractions, but instead, let them float by.

At this early stage in the process, allow the creative journey to unfold, rather than forcing ideas. Forcing stops the creative flow. Rather, move into a timeless state. It is all now. This is not the time to get hung up on the activities of the process, the "doingness" or how of it. Rather, it is a time to hold an idea, to explore possibilities, to develop the hint of a plan... and then let go.

If you'd like to try this right now, go ahead. Prime the pump. Ask yourself questions. Note the contrasts in your life. Are they emerging out of a crisis or perceiving grass greener on the other side of the fence? Where do they reside on your emotional scale? Record them in lists. Use as many pages as you wish. I've included thirty spaces below. Feel free to keep adding as many items as you wish. Remember how I had twenty careers in mind when I did an exercise like this with Ben? Our first job is to focus on what we want, why we want it, what it will look like, how we will feel, and what we will do with it once we have it. That's why Ben had me write more and more information about each of the ideas. Excluded from our lists are worrying about how we will do it or when we will get it, or overanalyzing the potential journeys between where we are and where we want to be. As one of my mentors put it, "How is none of your business."

My Want List

What do I want?

Why?

How will I feel when I have it?

1. _____

2. _____

3. _____

4. _____

5. _____

6. _____

7. _____

8. _____

9. _____

10. _____

11. _____

12. _____

13. _____

14. _____

15. _____

16. _____

17. _____

18. _____

19. _____

20. _____

21. _____

22. _____

23. _____

24. _____

25. _____

26. _____

27. _____

28. _____

29. _____

30. _____

With multiple options before us, our next task will be to prioritize them. Ben helped me do that by asking me to eliminate some ideas as I added more detail to my original list. Ultimately, we reach a point where we *decide* to pursue one of them through our actions. If we do not make that decision, they will remain only wishes.

Not surprisingly, at the point of crisis after the landslide, we were extremely focused mentally and emotionally. We knew exactly what we wanted—a home to reunite our family—and the resources, clues, and insights came to us relatively quickly. However, finding the rental house was only the first, relatively simple, step in the rebuilding process. Purchasing a new home was the next step we could see. It felt like a distant goal, but it would happen step-by-step, each step revealing the next until they became more than steps. The steps would become accomplishments. More would be revealed once we got there.

What we did not realize at the time was that recovery from a catastrophe, habitual activity pattern, or any loss is not just a physical event. It is colored by a range of thoughts and emotions that we have to explore before we can move past the experience into something new. If you've ever cleaned out a closet and had new, positive experiences soon after, you can understand that holding onto raw, buried emotions and old habits is like keeping a closet full of old clothes and items that no longer serve you, but you still keep them around. For some reason, they are comforting even if they are in the way. Often, we are not even aware of them. Hidden at a cellular level, after a serious illness or any other life-altering events that affect us, they have a way of demanding attention on their own, regardless of what we may be consciously planning.

My father had been a psychologist, so I was aware that depression could slip in unawares. I asked a friend Sue at church, who is also a psychologist, "When does depression hit?" She told me that it could happen at any point between six weeks and "whenever," and then shared a valuable bit of information designed to prevent the need for medication to deal with depression. She gave me a list of activities to do every day.

These activities would provide structure and emotional support if I became depressed. They were designed to ensure that I would take good care of myself physically (eat well, sleep enough, get exercise), to lift my spirits emotionally (laugh daily, be in beauty, or meditate), to ensure that I would grow mentally (learn something new), and to connect me with a supportive friend. Eventually I added one more of my own—be of service and give to others.

Today I would call these *key performance activities* (KPAs) that help us attain a healthy, well-balanced life. Through reworking Dr. Brothers's exercises over the years, I have learned that my version of such a life requires that I spend time on my relationships, in a community or workplace, with friends, family, and spouse; that I have meaningful work that contributes to my sense of physical and financial well-being; that I maintain my physical surroundings as sacred, enjoying time in nature and with animals, in order to recreate myself regularly; and that I put my relationship with my higher power at the very head of this list. These KPAs make up the daily, consistent actions required to successfully maintain progress through the creative process. They are the first parts of a universal system of time and space that is based on repetition. Continual repetition of thought and subsequent actions form definite patterns, which are then taken over by cosmic habitforce and made permanent. If we choose what strengthens and rebuilds our willpower, we move our daily habitforce in a positive direction. Failure to choose well can shift habitforce in the opposite direction and put us in a downward spiral to serious depression or physical destruction. Humanity has been given the ability to choose which habits we will embrace through the shape of our thoughts and subsequent actions, but once established, they are very difficult to change.

There is a dynamic and creative nature to the energies you feel when you decide to pursue a purposeful goal. We were in love with our idea of a new house and felt the urge to move forward in pursuit of it. We had decided to follow this course until successful. Even with all the challenges facing us, we found ourselves moving into action without really thinking about it. We got into action even if we were a little slower than usual.

In the aftermath of the slide, I found that I enjoyed being part of groups with structured activities designed to help me heal without having to understand anything; just show up, participate, and help others. The shock of the landslide and significant loss we experienced left us with little resiliency.

Everything in my personal world was topsy-turvy and unsettled. Squatters needed to be removed from the damaged house. Stress was at astronomical levels, with no scheduled time for resolution. Everything was an unknown as we created on multiple levels—income, health, family, legal resolutions, finding a new home, and I began to realize, allowing myself to reevaluate the focus of my work. The desired results were anything but clear. At times, we were overwhelmed by so much to process, and that made persistent activities even more important. When all else appeared to be failing, I could fall back on simple, defined tasks to accomplish, even if I did not understand their value. I didn't have to know anything or believe anything. I just had to do the work as told until I was strong enough to plan again.

I learned that even simple tasks like making a bed or washing dishes can be difficult willpower exercises for those who are suffering. Motivational psychologist Heidi Grant Halverson spoke about willpower as a muscle that can be depleted; however, with rest and simple exercises, it can bounce back. I needed to find ways to exercise my willpower without overworking it. Building it up was important. Without it, I could amble around, my mind dreaming of our new house or lamenting our existing situation. Without the power of the will, we would not decide to do anything and then choose to act. If we were to move toward our next goals, it was critical.

We had already seen how the decision to get back to work after the landslide had helped us. And I had seen how the power of one decision could move me into a new career when I worked Dr. Brothers's exercise as a young woman. We needed willpower to make choices—choices to unleash the power of the universe around our intentions. My willpower was to be strengthened by regular participation in groups. All I had to do was show up.

CHAPTER 4

BUILDING THE BRIDGE FROM HERE TO THERE

I have to admit that in those first few months, we may have had a purpose, but our plan was pretty vague. We were still reeling from the feeling of complete powerlessness in the face of Mother Nature. For the short term, I was living a progressive journey. I had not yet connected the dots. I did not know that I had even "asked" for a solution. One of the first lessons I had to learn was to accept the things I could not change. Thankfully, I already had profound faith in source energy, a power greater than myself—and that copy of *There's a Spiritual Solution to Every Problem* I had carried with me from the house.

Early on in the book, Dr. Dyer talks about the importance of surrender, accepting that we do not know how to resolve a situation and then turning it over to the life force that keeps things running in the universe. It was in the process of "letting go and letting God" that I had had the curious sensation of having my hand held. I had experienced those earlier God shots—our magi in San Diego, finding the rental house, and a landslide attorney. If I could only remember to trust that guidance and take appropriate action, all would be well, but the process was still incomplete.

It was time to move into the next stage, what is often called bridging the gap. For me, the phrase bridge the gap always conveyed a monumental task that is extremely difficult to accomplish. Time and again, a sense of hopelessness accompanied the realization that we did not know how to do it and we did not know where to look for the solution. Yet bridging the gap between where we were and where we wanted to be was exactly what we had to do to move our lives forward after the disaster.

We began by taking an inventory of the assets we already had before we knew what we needed in order to move forward. It's a common enough practice in business to take an inventory; however, in the aftermath of the landslide, ours was far more than just a physical count. It proved to be holistic, demanding physical, emotional, mental, and spiritual attention as we relived what we had lost, saw what remained to build upon, and defined what we would need to recreate our lifestyle. In the first fog of the landslide, we felt ill-prepared. The shock, the enormity of it all, the financial question marks, and the physical requirements hid any workable solutions from view. We had no emergency kit to grab nor emergency guidelines to consult. (With all the value gained from 20/20 hindsight, I think ahead for emergencies now to make sure that we have a crisis checklist of what needs to fly out the door with us with very little warning. It's so much easier if you know where those items are so that they can be moved with you quickly.)

We made few decisions. We saved everything we could, boxed it, and put it into storage. We borrowed cameras and photographed everything, sure that it would somehow matter for insurance purposes. Once you are safe, the next instinctive question is who can help, who can you call? Among the people to contact: family, friends, your church, network and community assistance groups, your employer, your attorney, insurance, Goodwill Industries, and the Red Cross (www. redcross.org), which has helpful information on surviving disasters. Note that I did not suggest calling for government assistance first. Ironically, the most difficult aspects of my recovery came at the hands of the various bureaucratic agencies I had to encounter. I did not have an attorney at the time of the slide and only came to understand how important it would be after the fact. I am so grateful for the attorney who came to our assistance. I was able to hand off the majority of the bureaucratic angst. I imagine that is why I maintain a membership in LegalShield today. It is a legal plan that provides access to legal advice without having to worry about retainers and high hourly rates. "Worry less, live more" is their motto, and I have firsthand knowledge of how important that can be.

After a catastrophe, all our routines are destroyed. It is one of our first instincts to reestablish them as quickly as possible. I have also found that in the midst of all the disruption, avenues open for new opportunities to emerge. It is not necessary to look for them. They appear all on their own as we go through the salvage process. So as soon as possible, we went home to rescue whatever we could still save, armed with moving boxes, trash bags, tape, paper for lists, plastic sleeves, and Sharpies. This is the beginning of the inventory process, if only to locate what you need during the relocation phase, but it can be heart-wrenching to look at the damage and document it with photos, videos, and lists. It's physically exhausting as well.

Some can be saved, but much will need to be replaced. And this is one of the first moments of empowerment that I would not have known or cared about at that time. There are items we absolutely need, but there are others that are a matter of choice. It gives us the opportunity to decide what our life will be like moving forward. We are surrounded by many things that represent our past. We are always in the process of becoming something else, and there is no need to carry the past into the future if it no longer serves. However, each of us has our own moments when we are comfortable releasing the past. It takes time and may not happen at this particular moment of critical opportunity. Peter and I took a physical inventory, releasing nothing for at least a year and a half. Some things were not released for almost three years. And much to our surprise, we discovered several boxes stored away seven years after the slide.

We wanted to be able to ask the questions: What's still working in our lives? What isn't? Until then, we had to store everything while we determined what had to happen next, what was coming to us as a result of the landslide, and what problems were emerging because of governmental bureaucracies and regulations.

Once we were moved into our longer-term, transitional home, we settled into the emotional reverberations of the experience. It was a grief journey. Our shocked numbness protected us from being overwhelmed by the magnitude of our loss for the first few weeks. But then we felt the raw sensitivities of loss. We were grappling to find solutions that did not seem to be at hand. I had no way of knowing how to wrap my head around the size of our problems.

It's a point at which our attitude, how we feel about the situation, can either freeze us in our tracks or inspire us to take immediate action. Fortunately, we were immersed in a supportive community. We had others with whom to share our frustration and sorrow. We had others to help us find solutions. Within four months, we had started to adjust. Our physical symptoms lessened. Peter's back was better. I could lift the coffeepot. We settled into a regular lifestyle that provided for our security and allowed us to start to work on the very real practical and financial problems involved in reconstructing our world. We accepted what had happened on many levels and began to turn our attention to rebuilding our lives out of the chaos.

Recounting the story endless times, I came to call the landslide "life-altering." Not only was the physical destruction devastating; it was physically and emotionally time-consuming. I had to relive my emotions frequently as we prepared for a lawsuit against the city. Memories dredged up about my parents' drinking became the impetus to examine whether I might follow my mother's patterns unless I faced them head-on by making some lifestyle changes. I began to question my work in production and even went so far as to take an online MAPP Motivational Qualities Report (similar to the tests my dad had me score as a child). The results shook the dust off my thoughts about what motivates me: wanting to share ideas that help others to make a positive difference in their lives, training them through words, either written or oral. It reminded me of my thoughts about the retreat center.

Once again, I was revisiting the creation process, although not aware of it consciously. Provided structure through a set of simple tasks, repeated on a consistent, persistent basis, my emotional life shifted. Fear and anger were replaced with action and gratitude as we turned our attention to defining the future. I was using an achievement mindset, in which my thoughts and actions were proactively focused on achieving goals and moving forward, rather than just being reactive to whatever came my way.

The majority of our emotional work was done while we were in the Pink Palace, awaiting the outcome of the financial issues that would determine how we could move forward. Dr. Dyer mentioned the work of Dr. David Hawkins (author, *Power vs. Force*) in his books, and while recuperating I began to read it. Over twenty years of investigation, Dr. Hawkins developed a calibrated scale of consciousness based on his research in applied kinesiology (muscle testing), with direct correlation to emotional experience. On this scale, lower calibrations correspond with heavy emotions, such as despair, depression, and anger. The highest calibrations are connected to love and bliss.

What Hawkins was able to document was that as people change their feelings, shifting calibrations up or down on the scale, they perceive things differently. They experience the effect of attracting different things into their lives according "to where they're coming from" (*Power vs. Force*, Hawkins, p. 242). Using prison inmates in an identical environment as an example, Hawkins described those individuals whose slower energies created a world of despair, anger, guilt, and fear. Conversely, others with higher energies found courage, possibility, and transformation. The idea that we could affect results by paying attention to our thoughts and emotional reactions intrigued me. Imagine, if you will, that you could take a situation as emotionally distressing as a landslide, apply a series of questions and possibility thinking to the situation, and experience emotional relief that raised your overall feelings about what had happened. It can be and is done regularly in personal development work. Imagine that you could learn to do this by adjusting your thinking about all the conditions present in your life. Wouldn't you be enthusiastic about learning how it works? Wouldn't your enthusiasm carry into your daily life, so that you were eagerly anticipating what was coming next? It was the beginning of my move into a mental inventory.

Reviewing skills, interests, and past experiences is a mental exercise. It makes up the inventory of the nonmaterial assets we bring into any new venture, be it a personal tragedy or one we are taking on by choice. In the aftermath of the landslide, it became clear that the production work I had been doing had lost some of its luster. Production management is on the operations side. Rarely did I feel that I was contributing to the creative content. I was feeling a strong contrast between supporting the creative ideas of others and creating my own content.

Yes, I was still on the road to my vision of producing in a highly creative environment. Yes, I was still joking about retiring to work in a space where people explore their dreams. However, the two seemed mutually exclusive. I was exploring possibilities that seemed unrelated to my work.

It might be a good place to mention that the most challenging part of telling this story is that life's process is not linear, even though we would like to impose a straight story line onto it. In many ways, we try to see our lives the way they are crafted for a movie: three acts, beginning, middle, and end. We want all the pieces to come together so it makes sense to us while we, the audience, are watching it. But life is not like that.

Nor is life made up of very many breakthrough moments. Jeff Olson (author, *The Slight Edge*) speaks about this. He feels that people want to jump from story point to story point, breakthrough to breakthrough, rather like thirty-second montages in a film. We want to skip over the vast majority of our day-to-day progressive activities in life. They are not exciting. In fact, the activities that add up over time to build results are rather mundane.

Life could better be described as a spiral, cyclical and rhythmic by nature. Events, experiences, and knowledge gained on one turn of the spiral may jump across and become meaningful on the next turn at a higher level. We may not know the value of any chain of events until further along in the process. So, in the course of taking an inventory of our skills and abilities, it is useful to map out all the skills and job requirements you've ever had. Then, as you rebuild, you will be able to see which ones can transfer naturally into your next endeavors.

One of the best books I've encountered on this subject is *What Color Is My Parachute?* by Richard Bolles. As we tend to wear blinders about our own value to others, if you have the possibility to work with a coach or a mentor, you may benefit from their perspective. In my case, I worked with a coaching colleague, Kate, who used this technique to help me discover that coaching and production utilized the same skill sets. It was not such a wild leap from one to the other as I had imagined. What was I learning? There were, of course, the key performance activities recommended by my friend Sue S. that I mentioned earlier. Another friend, Marilyn L., introduced me to the online "Flylady," who taught her daily household routine to help bring order and self-discipline into my home.

With fear only a hair's breadth away from my consciousness, I was given another coincidental connection, a God shot. While sitting at a meeting, a young man shared that he had been told that all life boiled down to the following: "God is. God will. Do the work. Be of service." Say it another way: Source energy is. Life force is. Life force will express itself. It was so simple, capturing the existence of consciousness and its innate desire to grow and expand. I never saw him again, but his simple share has stayed with me ever since. Whenever I had doubts or fear push their way to the surface, I repeated those phrases and then took actions to do the work and be of service in complete trust.

The only respite I had from the monumental stress was to surround myself in group work every day. I fulfilled my role in church activities. I fulfilled my role with the Producers Guild Seminar Committee. By far, the most important thing I learned was the value of regular, daily association with others to achieve a common goal. I immersed myself into a routine, showing up every day, then letting go and letting God do the rest. I studied every day. I gained strength through positive associations and discovered the value of willingness. I surrounded myself with others who wanted calmness, serenity, and hope in their lives. I joined others in working the twelve steps, both in person and through the writings of others, and once again I was involved in taking an inventory. I recited the twelve steps each day, as if they were prayerful affirmations.

I learned the serenity prayer, which helped me to manage my emotions. I came to believe in a deeper way and strengthened my faith. It was a lesson in humility, patience, and forgiveness. I learned about the value of gratitude. I learned to turn over the anger, fear, doubt, worry, and resentment associated with all the issues of the landslide and other life-history events to my higher power, praying for resolution of conflicts and contrasts.

Above all else, I sought to grow in conscious contact with this higher power through prayer, meditation, listening, observing, and writing. And I listened to a still voice within during centered prayer that guided me to explore my dream visions, to set intentions, to play with a plan for their attainment, and to take the actions that would move me toward them.

Philosophies I had put aside in the five years since Vivian's death reappeared with new language that seemed to apply in more practical ways. I came to understand that all life vibrates at its own rate. We cannot control how anything or anyone else vibrates. If we resonate with what we desire, we will find it in our environment. If we don't like those results, then we need to do whatever it takes to shift that vibration. And that is done by repeating thoughts that match what we want. I read more of David Hawkins's books and listened to his audios, and learned that everything I desired was at the calibration of love, 500 and above on the consciousness scale.

As my emotional life stabilized and negative habit patterns were replaced in the wake of the personal work I was doing, I added the dimension of wanting to share the principles and process that enabled anyone to do this. I immersed myself in the study of these principles from multiple sources, and with gratitude for all the blessings I received, followed the paths that opened up before me. I watched for the lesson along each path. As I studied other systems, I found incredible similarities and subtle differences.

Most notably, in twelve-step programs, a group of people gather regularly to support one another in order to achieve a definite, common goal through a plan of persistent activity. The group holds the idea of positive achievement even while an individual may not see the possibility of such a reality.

This is exactly what Napoleon Hill gives us as the four components to accomplish our visions: focused attention on a very big why (purpose), a believable plan for how to attain it, and a mastermind group, defined as an alliance of two or more people cooperating in a spirit of harmony for the attainment of a definite purpose (*The Master Key to Riches,* Hill, p. 87), to support us and close the door against all negativity and obstacles, no matter their origin, that might serve to undermine our ability to accomplish the goal.

In this less well-known book, Hill explained that the most important aspect of achieving or creating success was not in the specifics, but in the self-discipline being acquired through the process. The price is vigilance, determination, and persistence. And how do we develop the self-discipline required? Hill is clear. *The sole method* is to focus persistently on one's "definite major purpose until Cosmic Habitforce takes over and begins to translate it into its material equivalent" (*Master Key to Riches*, Hill, p. 174).

The source of that persistence comes from carrying through on a plan and purpose as they operate through the mind. So many "idly float upon the tides of circumstances" (*The Master Key to Riches,* Hill, p. 212) in daily life. "No real effort is made. It has been easier to let things go as they will rather than exert the will to direct them." Isn't it fascinating that "the dividing line between success and failure is found… where aimless drifting ceases and our Definite Major Purpose begins?"

It's amazing how few of us know that the power of the mind controls a deliberate creative process. Since everything begins with a thought and those thoughts have the ability to move us toward a goal or completely away from it, it behooves us to know how the mind works and what that means to us. In rebuilding, we want to look at the thoughts, ideas, and information that have filled our minds in the past. Those things make up our philosophy about what is valuable, where we will place our time, how we will respond to adversity, and the conclusions we will draw. How did those ideas get in our heads?

We were conditioned by the thoughts of our family, friends, schools, neighbors, news anchors, books, movies, and advertising. Part of addressing adversity is "popping paradigms"—the thought habits that no longer serve us—as Sandra Daley called it in her book *Pop Your Paradigms*.

Renowned speaker Jim Rohn also spoke on that subject. He said that how we respond to adversity is far more important than the adversity itself. After a life-altering event, it is not uncommon to see people change. It certainly happened to me and to dear friends. Surviving seems to open us up to asking whether our conditioning and circumstances are working for us or against us. Life becomes too precious to allow ourselves to be controlled by something or someone else. We want to take charge of setting the sail in our lives, so we review our past experiences and learn from success and failure what worked and what didn't. We gain an objective appraisal from others who can see what we cannot. We evaluate what in our lives serves us to accomplish our goals. We watch for information and model the successes of others. And when we have gleaned enough, we use that information to dare to design what our ongoing vision will be by crafting an action plan for moving forward.

An action plan is more than a to-do list of actions to take. It is also a definition of what has to happen, beliefs we need to create in order to sustain our progress toward our goals, the core commitments we are willing to make on a daily basis to achieve our dreams, and an indication of the stepping-stones and mile markers by which to mark our journey.

We all need a plan in order to progress to each next step. I prefer to start with a game plan, something that provides some perspective on the overall progress that has to take place—as if I have a bird's-eye view of the path. The point of calling it a "game" is to infuse the design with joy and spontaneity. Have fun, lighten up, and access your intuition and creativity. The goal in this early phase is to create a plan for all the stages of your vision and identify where to start and at least one action that you can take right now to move forward. When you have a few accomplishments (or if you hit a brick wall), you will want to pause to review the results. Evaluating whether your actions have you on course allows you to adjust your plan, if necessary.

"Let's pretend" is the important phrase here. It's important to realize that you may not know all the elements of your game when you sit down to design it. It takes some time to research the broad strokes that will be required. The details will be revealed later as you move through the game.

Ha! As I write this, I realize that our version of the game plan was a business plan. I had awakened one night when fear was clamoring to be let into my mind, and an infomercial was on the television. It was for National Grants Conference, advertising an upcoming event. I was not evaluating whether it was a scam or not. I wanted the hope that it promised that we could get through our financial crisis. When all was said and done, they wanted us to write a business plan for Caravan West. Filling in their templates, we organized our plan around our vision of the new ranch:

Objective: We believe it is possible to move to our own, larger ranch, where Caravan West can expand.

Daily Commitments: Continue doing our normal day-to-day activities, that is, going to work and caring for our house, gardens, and animals. Do something every day toward accomplishing a milestone.

Milestones:

_____ Get rid of the old house.

_____ Obtain funds to buy a new one.

_____ Find the right property, with a homeowner willing to work with us while our financial issues resolve.

_____ Move to the new ranch.

_____ Recreate our lifestyle.

_____ Build our Western town.

Although we had calendar dates in mind, so much was out of our control that we chose to emphasize accomplishment rather than make deadlines. The one thing we could do "right now" was to design the ranch, roll the dice, and start moving around the game board. The game was on.

CHAPTER 5

CLAP YOUR HANDS
IF YOU BELIEVE

Have you ever seen the Mary Martin version of *Peter Pan*? I grew up with it and performed the title character myself. One of the most powerful moments in the entire show is when Peter's beloved fairy, Tinker Bell, is dying from poison. In those few moments, Peter turns to the audience in desperation, calling for their assistance to save her life. "If you believe, clap your hands!" And incredibly, every night, the audience begins to clap. It starts with a single person, then a few scattered across the auditorium until the entire space is ringing with loving support for the tiny flickering light in the lantern. Tinker Bell rallies, and her light flashes across the stage as everyone celebrates, even if this is only occurring in the suspended reality of the theater. We all want to believe that we can alter outcomes. When we believe that something can happen, we also expect it.

There is power in expectation. Bob Proctor recorded a program on the Law of Attraction in which he states that desire and expectation are the two phases of creation. Desire is possibility "within" seeking expression "without" through your actions. Proctor goes so far as to call expectation the triggering mechanism and calls upon each of us to learn to use the power of our minds to cultivate expectation around our desires. What happens when you expect something to happen? You believe—which triggers action.

The challenge for each of us, even when we have studied the creative process, is to believe and expect when our outer circumstances indicate the polar opposite and we have absolutely no idea how something will happen. In our deliberate process, we may have to create belief out of thin air. One of the ways that is accomplished is by taking small actions that move crazy ideas into possibilities.

Unwittingly, Peter and I began this process when we were sitting in the Pink Palace with huge expenses and insufficient financial resources to go forward or backward. Rebuilding the house, if it could even be done, was estimated conservatively at well over a half million dollars because of the engineering required to retain a mountain. Buying a new home required a significant down payment, and even staying where we were was costing us double our previous expenses for the two house payments and insurance. It would be a year and a half before there would be any resolution to the legal issues, and the results were impossible to predict.

The only course of action that gave us any comfort at all was to start behaving as if we were going to buy a new house. And that's what we did. We began to create our idea of our dream ranch. Every weekend we would comb the real estate listings for what was available. We'd take rides into the country together looking. We got a feel for the neighborhoods we liked and where we felt we could get the most bang for our yet-to-materialize buck. It felt good. It was easy. We were enjoying stress-free window-shopping. It turns out relaxed activity is a key component. Doesn't everyone do that? I believe those who manifest their dreams do, whether they are consciously aware of it or not.

When we began the weekly drives, we did not have a clear idea of what our lives would be like when we moved. It was in the process of visiting these towns week in and week out that we came to have a mental picture that we could carry with us all the time. We knew how long the commute would be. We knew the shops and restaurants that would be close-by. This image gave us a frame of reference to build our lives around.

A few years after the landslide, I purchased the audio program *The Science of Getting Rich* presented by Michael Beckwith, Jack Canfield, and Bob Proctor. In one of those lessons, Canfield tells a story that is an example of a deliberate use of this technique to accomplish a desired effect. The story was of a man who promised to pay the college education of every child who graduated from high school in a particular southern community. He didn't just make an idle promise. As Jack tells it, the man understood that those children had no idea what a college education meant or what it would be like. They had no way to visualize, let alone believe and expect that it was possible to graduate and go to college. So plans were made to take each child on a field trip to shadow a college student for a day. When they came home, they had something to build their belief around. And an amazing number of students completed high school and had their educations provided by that benefactor.

The same effect may have been at work when I was learning to fly on the trapeze or when direct sales organizations serve as role models as they teach how to sell products by sharing success stories with their trainees.

Once Peter and I had an image of the ranch we wanted, we began to do everything in our power to act as if we were moving into that house. This is another powerful technique to support your belief in something that has not yet manifested in your world. For us, it was doing everything we could to prepare to move, even though we still did not have the money and no way of knowing if it would materialize. We made an offer on the ranch, explaining our situation exactly. We pulled moving checklists off the Internet and began to organize what would have to happen when we were given the green light. We began to pack what made sense to pack. For months, everything dragged on. Even though we reached a settlement with the city, nothing was clear. We had no specific date for when we would receive payment. We were even fearful that it would all fall apart and we would be back to the dreadful situation in which we had lived for all that time. And then, after four months of delay, payment from the city came through. We were "made whole," freed from the old expenses and able to make the down payment we needed in order to close on the ranch. I am extremely grateful that I have always been blessed with a great deal of faith. My friends called me courageous; however, I have come to feel that courage is really the support of faith expressed in action. When I undertook this journey, I was not armed with any tools to consciously do this. Even as I began to tell this story, I had to stop and explore what the process of creating belief in a desired outcome entails, especially when there are no outer signs to support that belief. Prayer without action is merely wishing. Faith without works fails.

Here's the dilemma. Our minds—our subconscious minds—are set up to protect us from discomfort, failure, and danger. If we do not believe that something is safe or possible, we will not take action. When faced with something new, out of our normal activities with unknown or even perceived risk, the subconscious will protect us from ourselves. We may know intellectually that the desired outcome will be a great benefit or improvement in our lives, but we have some work to do to bring our subconscious on board. It's an odd feeling. Everything we may be dreaming about is only an action away, and yet we are paralyzed. We start to pursue the dream, then stop and turn tail, retreating to our previous situation. It is the moment the subconscious rejects a goal because of its operative paradigms. When we hit this wall, the way to move ahead is to use the conscious mind to build belief on one hand and create experiences and images for the subconscious mind on the other. Thankfully, we have an array of techniques to help us bring our subconscious on board. Thomas Alva Edison, the inventor, felt that imagination was the most powerful of our mental faculties, partly because it had the ability to help us get past our outmoded beliefs and habit patterns, called paradigms, by helping us to visualize a positive outcome. We've already spoken about how we first start with an idea, a vision of what we desire, and then focus our attention on it. People do it all the time to accomplish anything, even if they don't know that they are engaging in the creative process. I don't believe any movies or television programs could exist if people didn't work through that process. We certainly used it in getting our home.

We began to layer details into our vision. We wrote down a checklist of the rooms and amenities we wanted in our new ranch, like an order form, which we used to evaluate each house's asking price. We had a sense of the things that would have to happen in order for us to accomplish our goal, including preparing for the lawsuit, finding a new home, and preparing all the details of a move. It was a sketchy action plan at the time, but it served the purpose. Those simple visions were enough to access the energies that moved everything into place to help us get our ranch. At the time, we did not know how important it was to articulate what we wanted to feel when we got our new ranch, but our joint field trips together were filled with the emotion of expectation, the dreaming about how we would use the space, and the wonderful ways that we could enjoy our new home. We knew why we wanted certain features more than others. We knew the benefits we would gain when we had a space for all of Peter's collections, the horses, and ourselves. Now, I know that we were living the concept of organized planning. We were organizing our energies and our efforts around a purpose and a plan.

My personal struggles centered on the fears and emotional roller-coaster rides that came with the unknowing for such a long time. I had no tools, no process, and no system. I had not yet learned that vision needed to be armed with knowledge, good systems, and belief to lead to results. That might have made the journey less painful. Getting into our new ranch was not the end of the story. Even as I expressed gratitude for the many blessings we received regularly, something else was preparing to unfold. However, I had no idea where it was taking me. Although creating our new ranch appeared to be the most important goal at the time, the reality is that new opportunities were beginning to surface for both of us: Peter's business was about to get a boost, and I was about to give myself permission to help others identify and create their dreams. As our focus shifted from crisis mode to possibility thinking, the process was simple enough for children: play, fantasize, and allow one's imagination to create.

I have a dear friend Beverley who asked me if this process is not just fantasy. Yes, it is fantasy… that has the power to change worlds. It is the process of becoming what does not yet exist… of slipping into an alternate reality, beyond time and space. It is the world of the screenwriter or novelist, where one may write a scene and then tear out the pages and create a different reality. It is accomplished through journaling, scripting, musing, or "praying rain," a method reminiscent of rainmakers who summoned rain by "becoming" the rain themselves. It is accomplished by hypnosis and "quantum jumping," a technique developed by Burt Goldman to utilize the skills of hypnosis and theories of parallel universes beyond our own to meet our "doppelgangers," exact duplicates of ourselves with skills we desire.

But how is this possible? Why would such processes work? As we prepared to move onto the new ranch, my journey was about to take a turn centered on the creative power of the mind.

"Ask, and you will receive; seek, and you will find; knock, and the door will be opened" (Matt. 7:7).

"Then leave the job of bringing it about to the Infinite Intelligence of your subconscious mind" (Dr. Joseph Murphy, *Think Yourself Rich*, p. 14)

CHAPTER 6

SUITING UP FOR THE NEXT-PRESENTED THING

I remember awakening the morning of July 1, 2006, with an incredible sense of relief. We had gotten through the aftermath of the landslide and were now living on a five-acre ranch with a beautiful view in a lovely community, with ten acres of wildlife corridor across the way. Astounding! We had ample space to spread out, both for the horses and for Peter's collections.

I was in production on a reality television show, so there was not much time to ponder the changes ahead just yet, except to look around with profound gratitude and some disbelief. First, we went through an extended period of waiting for the other shoe to drop. It was impossible to believe that this lovely space was our new home. Every day I would give thanks and pray that this feeling would last for a couple of years. With catastrophe behind us, we could focus on what we wanted. While I was away each day, Peter was repeating that all-important first step in the creative process, 100 percent focused on creating his part of our vision—building his business in our new location by developing the ranch.

Once again, friends came out to help us relocate. This time, however, it was with the joy of helping to rebuild, the shared feeling of a community engaged in barn raising. Everything that had been hurriedly thrown into storage, plus household items surrounding us over the past eighteen months, had to be sorted and placed into their new home. It took one month to move everything onto the property. We completely filled the workshop that came with the property, which we affectionately called the Gray Whale, with a nod to the design center in West Hollywood nicknamed the Blue Whale.

After years of working out of a modest home and garage, Peter did not even discuss the next stage of his vision with me. Next thing I knew, he had happily acquired mini-barns to house his collections of stuff. Laid out in a large rectangle, they gave the appearance of a small town, which we named Peetzburgh, after a sign Peter found in a flea market back east. As the wife, it was great for me. For the first time, all the Western paraphernalia had display areas separate from the house. Even we were astounded by how much he had accumulated over the years and how we had lived with it all in such a small place.

Talk about having a place to putter! Peter was in hog heaven. We looked forward to new opportunities emerging. Peetzburgh was like a sculpture to be carved from the piece of mountain we had acquired. We gathered the materials around us and began to create anew. Within three months, display rooms began to emerge. Buckaroos with construction skills dressed each barn with a covered sidewalk, to which Peter added the barrels, chairs, and other artifacts of daily Old West living in a small town. Peter's vast collection of Western materials easily divided up to create dedicated buildings that caught the flavor of the Frontier West—a general store, bar, sheriff's office with jail, saddle shop, and horse corral. Costumes had their own barn, and the rest found housing in the workshop. After years of having every nook and cranny crowded with Western stuff, it was a dream come true to see fully dressed, themed display buildings in Peetzburgh. If we could provide locations for filmed projects as well, so much the better.

We were thrilled when we had our first opportunity to shoot a scene from a reality show on the property. However, with the arrival of that first film crew, we realized that we were missing a few features for great Western filmmaking. As the director scouted with his creative team, the critique came down. We were too close to neighbors, in line of sight of the power lines, with no place for long rides for stagecoaches or horse chases. The view was beautiful, but not quite a vista shot. Although we felt as if we were in the wilderness, to the trained eye, we were also at the edge of suburbia. It was hard to believe that within three months, we knew we needed a bigger solution.

This situation is a good example of a contrast. It represents the realization of a gap between where you are and where you want to be. When faced with a contrast, we are presented with a choice. Give up because the gap is too large, or accept the difference and set to work to bridge that gap. So once again, Peter and I would need to live our way through the gap, the imperfection in our realized vision, in order to develop a better situation. This is how the creative process works, ever seeking improvement and expansion. With one success newly in hand, we began the process again. The new house was not the end of the journey. There was more to develop. Peter's dream expanded. He wanted to be a go-to guy for the Old West, including locations. We would have to refocus and refine our vision.

Answers do not necessarily appear in an instant. We find that you have to continuously hold a vision with positive energy while you go through the motions of living in the other areas of your life. The problems that surface in daily life do not necessarily correspond to what you are consciously creating. And life had certainly changed after we arrived at the new ranch. Even if we were extremely grateful as we enjoyed our purchase, the space offered some new challenges.

I was adjusting to life in the country. Raised in the hothouse environment of suburbia, I expected city services to automatically be present. It took time to learn about propane tanks and the husbanding of wells. To this day, it is always a surprise if the water tank runs low because one of us has left the water running to the horse trough. My visions for landscaping needed to be put aside while we learned about providing water for plants in the high desert. After so many years in the Los Angeles area, I had forgotten about snow. The move from the valley took us up to a 3,300-foot elevation, which was just high enough to catch the occasional snowstorm. Within a short time, we were snowed in for the first time on our dirt road, where we depended on our neighbor's tractor to dig us out rather than city plowing services.

The horses loved the snow, even if I was rummaging through every bit of clothing I owned to find warm gloves and hats.

In short order, I learned to think through my shopping plans so that I could get everything I needed in one trip. After all, the major shops were nine miles away. With more land came more maintenance. There was brush to clear each year; fences to mend when the horses leaned against them; and coyotes, hawks, bobcats, owls, and rodents to deter from destroying property, livestock, and pets. We found it as important to maintain what we had already brought into our lives as it was to continue to expand our creations. The desert was harsher. Fire was part of the seasons here. Frequently we would sit at home looking out over the valley as flames crested valley walls opposite us, all our senses primed for action if they came too close to us.

As we discovered the challenge of living with what we already had created, we set out to adjust our long-term vision. The new ranch was a minimized version of our dream. In the original plan, we had joked about 170 acres (seventy for Peter's western town, seventy for me to build a retreat center, and thirty as a buffer between what seemed like such divergent worlds). In the real expression of five acres, we found a learning curve all its own. Fortunately, if what we see before us does not match the image in our mind, it does not define who or what we are. We are only in the process of becoming what we see in our minds. Look to nature. Does water stop when it hits hard rock? No, it seeks a soft spot and works over, under, and around until a path is found.

For fifteen years, hadn't I joked that when I retired I would run a center that would provide opportunities for people to discern direction in their lives through guiding, retreats, and quiet space? Now, in the aftermath of the slide, I experienced an impression of "if not now, when?" Was it time? Was I ready to retire from production? Did I know enough to do this? What did I need to do to find and manage such a space? Was I finally in the place where I could create an environment where people could explore their dreams?

I wanted to make it work on the new ranch, but sharing five acres with a western town and horses did not seem to lend itself to the development of the quiet retreat with the Western Zen atmosphere I had envisioned. Should I start to make our current home such a space through my landscape choices? I thought about gardens, walkways, and a labyrinth. I thought through what I could do right where I was. Did my vision run parallel to Peter's vision of the town? It was something to contemplate when I wasn't buried in production.

Peter and I had discovered over the years that working together was one of the best ways to achieve what we wanted to manifest. When we were pulling in the same direction, it was a perfect mastermind, reminding me of the horses that traveled across country with us so long ago. We hobbled them to a tire at night to keep them out of trouble. However, they were smarter than we were at the time. Eventually they learned that if they pulled that tire together in the same direction, they could run wherever they chose. Our method of hobbling only worked when they were pulling in opposite directions—or after we learned to tie the tire down.

We were working together to create something at our new home. The chance to film at our ranch was infrequent, so Peter was busy working on other film projects. This was great; however, the most wonderful opportunity came when he was introduced to a man with lots of acreage. As they developed a relationship, Peter gained the ability to use the larger ranch as a location for film, television, and other entertainment projects. It was the perfect alternative to the problems we were experiencing at our ranch.

As Peter's vision of the ranch continued to expand, I was playing with my own ideas about using the space in conjunction with a business-plan template. The idea kindled when I was back at work, growing into my line producing role. It was not a new idea but the one that had started when I helped my dad score tests in his practice—the one that continued to make its presence known in my psychosynthesis training and avocation over the years. It was that strong impetus to lead people through a process to recreate their lives in a new and positive way after a crisis by discovering what filled them with passion and enthusiasm.

When certain ideas become a thread that carries through many of our activities, teachers like Napoleon Hill and Bob Proctor, even pastor Rick Warren, define these as *purpose*: long-term, highly meaningful ideas that inform the choices we make throughout our lives. Peter and I do not necessarily share the same life purpose; however, one of the strengths in our marriage has been imagining and then granting each other the freedom to grow into our respective dreams. It is a mastermind—when two or more people are gathered for a common purpose, helping to create the belief required to maintain persistent activity. I am so grateful that we support one another through the ever-changing creative process. I must say that it is never dull.

CHAPTER 7

IMAGINE THE BOOTS

Over the past six years, while studying how the mind works in the creative process, I have seen that the nonconscious (or subconscious) is extremely powerful. It works in the background to create anything you have contemplated with strong, emotional desire. In my case, the landslide opened up an opportunity to place circumstances, situations, and resources in my path at a time when I was most receptive to receive them.

As you know, in short order, I had participated in the neuro-emotional work that opened me to wounds in my psyche, discovered centered prayer and twelve-step work, and reawakened that "crazy" idea about directing a retreat center or business incubator. So in my spare time between shows, it was fun to play with a business plan, completing a mission statement for a space that fit my vision. As I resonated with these new experiences, new possibilities emerged.

Of course, I had no credentials. Who would listen to me? I contemplated how I could redefine myself to create such a space. Since the concept had persisted for years, in the aftermath of the landslide, I was wide-open for my subconscious to start bringing new possibilities my way. I was not aware that the playful imaginings, the joy of the dream, and the details of a plan, all taking place internally, if connected through meaning with an external event could create a coincidence that would show me a way to redefine myself and gain credibility (Goswami, *God Is Not Dead,* p. 259). It was a moment of synchronicity.

Peter was absorbed with developing Caravan West Ranch when a flyer from a former psychosynthesis colleague arrived in our mailbox. I had had no contact with him since Vivian's death. The flyer was an invitation to participate in a coach training program he ran. I was too busy to do anything with it, but I wanted to give it some thought. That piece of paper kept reemerging at various spots on my desk for several months. Since that kept happening, I suspected there was a message in it for me. Simultaneously, e-mails began to arrive from an entertainment colleague who was now in the real estate business. The flyers described coaching as a career that could meet my major needs: enough income to support me and work that served my dream. Could this be the training I needed to build the retreat center? It was something worth checking out. Conservative by nature, I began by reading a book about coaching.

By the time I had finished it, I knew that I would love it. Even though my days were consumed by production, I decided to pursue coaching—or what is called "guiding" in psychosynthesis. Evaluating the coaching industry filled my free time for months before I finally enrolled in a program that felt right for me: Sharon Wilson's Empowered Spiritual Life Coach training. One of the key concepts of Wilson's approach was its emphasis on the techniques of inner work (like meditation), as well as the thinking, "pre-paving," and visualizations that set the stage for creating or finding solutions to personal and professional issues.

Working with our mentor facilitator, Fawn Christianson, and student colleagues, we spent months going through the program exactly as our future clients would. One of the first ideas I had to consider was the instruction to lighten up.

Another important idea I needed to personally integrate was that I have valuable skills and something worthwhile to offer others. When I first began to consider guiding anyone, I seriously questioned how I would be able to communicate this process to anyone else. It was one thing to talk about and use someone else's philosophy and techniques, but how could I tell people that "it works if you work it" unless I had seen the results myself? That question was to be a major stumbling point for me, sort of a catch-22 requiring personal experience. Even as I write this material, it is necessary to remind myself that I don't have to be a method actor. I don't have to live it all to understand and teach it. It can be as simple as using our creative intelligence, but I wasn't aware of that yet.

At one point, driving around with Peter, I asked myself, "What could I share that would help people in the depths of their despair? How could I help them to pull themselves up by the bootstraps if they have no boots?" And the answer came: "Imagine the boots." For me, it was one of those quantum leaps when the theory you have studied takes on a new meaning. Of course… everything begins with a thought. The "work" is to help people utilize their imagination as one of the most powerful of their intellectual faculties. The goal is to visualize the one thing we desire like a movie unfolding in our minds… a mind movie.

For the longest time I questioned whether I had very much talent in the visualization area. I didn't have any dream boards, with their collection of images, words, and colors on a board to reflect my desires. I hadn't made a mind movie on my computer to utilize visualization techniques that draw upon mental imagery and affirmations in a video context.

I knew what they were intellectually, but had not made them. Thankfully, I was able to hear Jack Canfield speak, and read New Thought student Genevieve Behrend's description about how visualization works so that I could later apply it consciously for myself. I want to emphasize the word *consciously* because the more I learned about this subject, the more I realized that my husband and I had accomplished quite a bit through dreaming or creative imagining without really knowing what we were doing.

We had written scripts about "caravanning" west, and then did it. As Peter's successes grew as an actor, we discovered he had another talent, and we developed his business, Caravan West, named after our movie script. My own career desires shifted from performing to producing, alongside a strong avocation for spiritual studies in what amounted to a dual path for years.

When that landslide hit in 2005, we were aware that we had outgrown our home. We envisioned a larger ranch for ourselves and the animals. The point in sharing these adventures is that Peter and I had been "imagining the boots" for years and backed up our imaginings with personal development materials.

What the coaching class was showing me was that desires are voiced on conscious and unconscious levels through our imagination. The key is not to stop there, but to focus enough to harness the power gained through using the imagination and then get ourselves out of the way. Think about the ranch again. When we first got the idea, it was fleeting, but as we played with it over the years, energy attached to it. At first the energy was sluggish, but as we continued to consider the concept, the energy increased, attracting more to it. The process is called "amping up" the energy by mentally visualizing and adding emotion to an image until we believe we can successfully create our vision, thus "activating" the ranch idea.

After the landslide, our dream, physical need, and emotional desire combined, bringing us to the point where we were ready to take action, challenge the beliefs that were stopping us, and step into it—go for it. We did not know how or if the ranch could happen or how we could overcome the financial hurdles, but we took all the next-presented steps because it *was* possible. Because there was so much uncertainty, we had to get out of our own way and let go, without concern for the outcome, in order to let it happen.

In class, Fawn would guide us through visualizations in which we used our imaginations. In one, I saw an auditorium filled with people who were all my ideal clients, filled with excited anticipation as they awaited my arrival for a presentation. I was able to imagine who they were, what they felt when I was there, and the joy I felt when they were with me.

In another guided meditation, I became aware that my center had become a symbol for the work I wanted to do. Initially, I interpreted it as a place where others could come to search for their lifework, but gradually I became aware that the physical location was less important than the essence of the guiding work: creating a space for others to explore the creative process. The first task was to bring the center to life within myself, after which multiple venues would appear that could serve the purpose—to share the creative principles. The retreat center would exist wherever I created that environment.

One of the first steps when undertaking deliberate creation is to become aware of the conditioning and thought habits, called paradigms, that prevent us from achieving what we defined for our vision. I had plenty of these beliefs that were getting in the way of my success. Many of them involved financial issues. I didn't want to waste money. I wanted to get out into the workplace faster, but I didn't like selling. I had no frame of reference for successfully raising millions of dollars. Once I was aware of the paradigms, then it became necessary to learn how to overcome them. We learned how to use the power of affirmations (positive statements), as well as progressive beliefs (moving from a state of disbelief to belief through revising regularly repeated affirmations). We learned the power of questions to stimulate the subconscious to become our greatest ally in this process. We learned to use these tools daily, to journal, and to voice statements out loud.

The class also made us aware that we may unwittingly overlook some older voiced desires or we may be unaware that we are holding something in our subconscious that has become more powerful than what we are consciously pursuing. These may surprise us by getting in the way or be experienced as negative experiences, circumstances, and environments.

During the program, I was first exposed to people who are currently applying creative principles. Most of them appeared in the film *The Secret,* discussing these "success" principles. It was also here that I first learned of Esther Hicks (coauthor, *Ask and It Is Given: Learning to Manifest Your Desires*), translating the thought forms of Abraham into words.

As I came to learn, in our modern era, many coaching programs and online studies are conducted via regular conference calls. Students call into a conference line, where they can listen to presentations, participate in exercises, and exchange comments about the work at hand. I would go into the production office early to listen to the weekly training calls before sending the crew out to shoot the reality schedule we had planned. The more I studied, the more I wanted to explore a new venture outside production that would mesh with my vision. What I was studying felt so good in contrast to reality shows.

Sharon Wilson had two strong suggestions: keep a journal for daily, early morning scripting, where we could write out whatever we wanted to create or experience that day; and carry a small notebook to use throughout the day as a place to vent in private. Although we are often counseled not to dwell on the negative when we are engaged in the creative process, there is a time and a place to express our feelings and ways to do it. Wilson developed "perceptual shift logs" so that we could manage our feelings when we were caught up in wild emotional shifts after a negative situation.

Basically, we can manage feelings by writing down all the details of what happened that caused us to feel emotional distress, or as Esther Hicks would translate it, "contrasts." Journaling helps to draw feelings, as well as creative thoughts, from the nonconscious part of our mind, offering us a way to connect to that very powerful aspect of our being. Once the emotional reaction has been acknowledged, we have the opportunity to shift gears, literally. "Moving up" to our conscious mind, our intellectual faculties can help us to think through the situation, asking questions of and obtaining answers from within. The journals take on a "conversational" aspect.

My personal journals are an important part of my daily routine to keep spiritually fit. The routine is based on the process Wilson recommended. Here is a rough idea of what I do:

- I align with my higher power, as I understand it, and all those on the physical and nonphysical planes who have contributed so much to who and what I am.

- I express gratitude for at least ten experiences that support my goals and positive feelings each day. That may translate into giving thanks for the dishes being washed, but the more I notice positive events in daily activity, the more there seem to be.

- I "pre-pave" or "script" how I would like the current day to go. It is as if the universe asks me each morning, "What do you want?" And I get the chance to answer.

- If my emotions need managing, I may take myself through a series of questions and answers to soothe them. What happened? How did it make me feel? How could it have been better? What would have to happen for me to feel better? What can I do now?

- This is followed by a series of positive questions and affirmations that ring true to me.

- I finish my journaling with a declaration like, "This or something better now comes to me. So be it, and so it is. Thank you."

- My signature is a doodle, capturing the joy, love, financial well-being, and goals I wish to achieve—and with a whoosh of desire, I turn over the day to my higher power and begin my day's activities. If I have received an impression to take a specific action, I make it a point to do it immediately.

Fawn and other people told me anecdotally, and I have found it to be true myself, that we do know what we want, even if we don't think we do. However, the subconscious mind may protect us based on older conditioning. To mine its treasure, we frequently have to sneak in the back door, asking ourselves, "If I did know, what would it be?" We make lists, write stories, draw, or paint. We play or participate in improvisation. We use a process of choosing one idea over another, or expanding on a few of the items on our list until we narrow down the possibilities to what we really want the most. Does it sound familiar? Yes, it is just like the exercises that Dr. Joyce Brothers and Ben Dolan described years ago.

Our homework assignments asked us to review our energetic blueprints and brainstorm. You've probably done it yourself when you break an overall vision into smaller components in a visual format. Think of something you are trying to organize right now. Since the mind thinks in pictures, sketch out your thoughts on paper. Write a word or short phrase on the paper and circle it. Then keep adding words and circling them, allowing each thought to lead into the next. When we brainstorm, there does not have to be a precise order. We allow one thought to lead into another randomly, writing as quickly as possible until we run out of free-flowing ideas.

From here, it is a short hop to organize all those ideas into a logical list of what we want (like an order form) and an action plan that supports our goals. An action plan lists the things you need to do in order to accomplish a goal in as much detail as you know at the time. Wilson kept her action plans to what could be accomplished in thirty days. It's fairly easy to "order up" a step that needs to be taken to move forward. However, we may need a more detailed focus on that step, during which we realize that there are several smaller steps that need to be taken to achieve it. Sharon Wilson calls this "chunking down" a goal into the specific actions that are needed. It's an important step that a great many people miss. I certainly did. I love thinking in grand scale, but progress depends upon the details.

When I completed the one-year program, I had grown personally, had a kit of tools to work with people, and had an understanding of the services that coaches use to reach out to others, but I didn't know what to do next. I could not figure out where to find clients, and my beliefs and paradigms about not being qualified still lingered. Two instructions repeated in my meditations: "Get it out there" and "Find a role model."

This is a good time to make the point that we may have a variety of visions that help us live our purpose. When our purpose seeks expression, the subconscious mind sends us multiple opportunities to live it. Locking in on one vision may prevent us from seeing other possibilities that could be better over time. So we have to stay open to the unexpected, making our way through a string of such choices called visions. Focusing on each vision in turn, we accomplish goals specific to each one until they weave together to achieve our purpose.

So with purpose in mind, I set off to find my vision of a role model. Over the next few years, I invested in numerous programs that matched my emerging idea of what I would like to do and the process I would like to share with others. My exploration read like a litany of the saints as they came into my awareness, and I studied their works and attended their lectures or trainings, including: Renae Bechthold, Ted McGrath, Bob Proctor, Jack Canfield and Michael Beckwith, John Assaraf, Gerry Robert, Marilyn Jenett, Brian Tracy, Burt Goldman, Mary Morrissey, John Maxwell, Abraham-Hicks, and others. Some were brief interludes; all offered gems to place in the treasure-house of my mind.

There was a basic core of information in the audio program *The Science of Getting Rich,* and by the time I had completed it, I was ready to choose Bob Proctor as my role model and trainer. Initially, the course work would be conducted via telephone, augmented by Bob's own home-study programs. Since it would take a week or more to receive my materials, Bob recommended a live weekend conference that was within a couple of hours of home. It was a celebration. Greg Reid and Sharon Lechter had just published *Three Feet from Gold,* inspired by Napoleon Hill's *Think and Grow Rich.* I was still very conservative with my use of funds, but I decided to throw caution to the wind and attend.

During their grand kickoff conference, my brain felt as if it were expanding beyond self-imposed limitations. It was a powerful entrée to the very heady world of personal development. I got to meet Bob in person that trip. I was introduced to the work of Loral Langemeier, Mark Victor Hanson, Les Brown, and many others. I reconnected with old friends, Frank and Carmel Maguire. Even participating felt like a huge stretch. The experiences were exhilarating! At each step along the way, I gleaned yet one more nugget of wisdom. The presentations were great. I was gaining knowledge, but I did not yet understand the power of the mind.

CHAPTER 8

THE MYSTERIOUS
ASPECT OF MIND

Mingling as we did at that conference, I heard many people refer to Bob Proctor as a coach's coach. For many who had worked with Bob in his world-class coaching programs, Bob had been the quintessential spokesperson for Napoleon Hill's book *Think and Grow Rich*, moving from $4,000 per year to a six-figure income in a year's time. He took what he learned from Hill's success philosophy and built a thriving business in several large cities before joining Earl Nightingale and Lloyd Conant in their well-known publishing company. Bob went on to publish his own book, *You Were Born Rich,* and founded his own seminar company. Just before I learned about him, Proctor had risen to prominence as a key presenter in the film *The Secret.* His work reached hundreds of thousands of people. For me, he exemplified the contributions a coach could make. As a role model, he set the bar pretty high.

To prepare for our upcoming master class with Bob, we were asked to study his courses, participate in training calls, and facilitate a mastermind group focused on Hill's book. I had been coaching a small group already and decided to incorporate *Think and Grow Rich* to provide some additional structure to our sessions. Each member received a copy of the book. We then planned our mastermind as Hill had instructed, meeting weekly.

Using a mastermind is an integral part of Hill's philosophy, one of four components needed in order to work consistently toward our goals.

Such a group, composed of individuals with similar philosophies and working toward a common goal, provides a regular, positive support system. Hill cited story after story of successful individuals who built industries based on this principle. Andrew Carnegie, for one, had a mastermind group of fifty individuals who helped him build US Steel and become the wealthiest man in the world at that time.

So we focused on the basics of Hill's book, one chapter per week. We had spoken about dreams and desires earlier. We had even attempted to create vision boards to help stimulate dreams that had been buried by several years of hard times. Yet it was not until the fifth week that the pieces began to come together: identifying each person's "one thing" that energized his or her passion, focusing attention on it, developing a believable plan, and taking actions using the group for support and as a barrier to all negativity and obstacles, no matter their origin, in order to hold that focus during the entire time it takes to accomplish one's goals. During that fifth week, something clicked, and Joelle D. got it.

Over the next few months, Joelle articulated her dream, researched what would be needed to go for it, and began the challenging task of applying to graduate school after many years outside academia. Her focus shifted from "why it can't" happen to "why it can." Resources flowed to support her desires, and she was accepted into a prestigious graduate school for a degree in arts management.

Having someone in our life that supports us is incredibly important. In our very self-sufficient society, we have a tendency to take pride in doing everything on our own. However, within the coaching community, there is a powerful statement—we have to do it on our own, but we cannot do it alone. In fact, the process of rebuilding our lives, the very tasks of survival, are shortened and less painful when we embrace relationships with others along the journey. Have you ever wanted to quit? Have you ever felt overwhelmed by the devastation and destruction of everything you have built up after it all fell apart? When you are feeling that way, it's a very good time to look at your support structure. Who is in it? Who are your associates?

Ironically, we may be surrounded by well-meaning friends and family who are not supporting our needs or dreams. Their personal goals may not match our own in that moment, so that the relationships tear upon one another. It's not that we throw them out of our lives. After all, we love many of these people. But we do have to learn how to lessen their impact and draw upon other resources to help us. Otherwise, the cumulative effect of negative mind chatter can undermine the accomplishment of our goals.

Not only do mastermind groups buffer us from the negativity around us, but they bring added power. Being with people who have shared experiences can help us through emotional and creative challenges. As is often the case with focused thought, as soon as you ask for a group that meets your needs, you will become aware of multiple possibilities. It is as if such support groups pop up everywhere. Someone will organize a group to address a common problem, and word will spread via the Internet, newspaper, e-mail, or watercooler.

Something happens when multiple brainpower is focused on a problem. The combined energy of brain cells creates another mind—a mastermind—representing the combined wisdom, experience, and knowledge of all the minds gathered in a harmonious manner for the accomplishment of a common goal. These goals can be as simple as learning a new skill, or as complex as creating a theme park, sending a man to Mars, or overcoming shared, personal problems. We see mastermind groups proliferating in the various twelve-step programs available, where the only membership requirement is that participants share a goal to overcome a common problem.

While waiting for Proctor's in-person training, I started a second group, working through his book with colleagues also seeking to build successful coaching practices. Each of us was, in some way, struggling to discover how to move from student to income-earning business owner. I shared a mind movie with this group. In it, I needed a bridge to cross a huge chasm. Approaching the chasm with feelings of fear and helplessness, I was guided to get on my hands and knees to approach the edge of the gap and peek over. Looking over the edge, I was startled to discover that there was a path in the side of the wall that led down into the ravine, where all the supplies for building a bridge were waiting. All I had to do was to climb down and start assembling the pieces. Or if I liked, I could just climb up a similar path on the other side. I did not need a bridge, although it would be helpful to those who followed behind me. What a relief! I scrambled down the path and began to take an inventory of the resources around me.

All my activities came to conclusion as Bob Proctor's master class approached. My work on the US Pavilion for World Expo in Shanghai was delivered. The mastermind groups completed their assigned books, and I was ready to jump into something totally new.

My colleagues in the upcoming study were each preparing their own seven-minute presentations on a core concept in Proctor's program—a picture of the mind. When Bob's mentor, Leland Val Van de Wall, shared such an image with him, it became the thread that connected what he had previously known with what became his success strategy.

The diagram, affectionately called "the stick person," is a model of the mind and body originated by the late Dr. Thomas Fleet of San Antonio, Texas, in 1934. Dr. Fleet founded the school of concept therapy, holding that since we think in pictures, we should build visual models for complex ideas. To deliberately build anything into our reality, we need an image that we can use to help us create whatever results we choose. Here is that diagram:

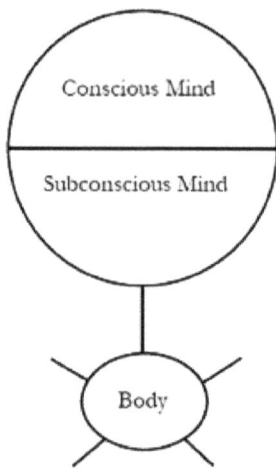

Stick person diagram of mind and body

The large circle representing the mind is connected to a smaller circle representing the body. The mind is larger, to reinforce the idea that our focus should be on the mind, rather than the body, even though the body is more obvious in our day-to-day experience. The larger circle is divided into two parts—the conscious and the subconscious mind. (This may remind you of Assagioli's egg diagram depicted earlier. They are both maps of consciousness.)

We are most familiar with the conscious mind. After all, that is where all the information we obtain through our senses is housed. This is the part of the mind that interacts with the outer world. We experience through our senses, and then utilize the six intellectual faculties mentioned earlier to think and engage in outer activity. *Perception* is our point of view, how we look at something. *Reasoning* provides us the ability to choose and build ideas. *Memory* enables us to store ideas and experiences that we can recall on demand. *Will* provides us the ability to hold an idea in spite of surrounding distractions. We pick up ideas and feelings beyond what come to us through our senses through *intuition*. And we put it all together through either *synthetic imagination* (rearranging old ideas, concepts, and plans into new combinations) or *creative imagination* (intuitive insights that lead to entirely new ideas and creations).

The conscious mind decides the type of life we want to experience. We may resist accepting this concept, but we become what we think about. For example, how many times have you reacted to a story in the news not with the question "What were they doing?" but with "What were they thinking?" On some level, we understand that our thoughts ultimately determine the results we get.

However, the conscious mind is only part of the mind. There are many other maps of consciousness that attempt to capture what exists in the nonconscious. Fleet's diagram is the simplest, rolling all the possible nonconscious permutations into one: the subconscious mind. To try to explain all the nonconscious layers would be the material for another book. In fact, my colleague Barbara Babish found that there were more than enough maps of consciousness to make a doctoral dissertation.

Using Fleet's diagram, we use one term, the subconscious mind, to describe the largest part of the mind. First, it makes up the autonomic nervous system, housed in the hypothalamus portion of the cerebellum and the brain stem, which physically runs the automated systems in the body, that is, circulation, breathing, the heart beating, and our healing (*The Power of Your Subconscious Mind*, Murphy, p. 99).

Numerous doctors, hypnotherapists, and body workers describe the subconscious mind's impact on our existence through memory and analysis as well, but it is the subconscious mind's impact on results, as described by Dr. Joseph Murphy, that is most important to the creative process. The subconscious calls the shots. We may decide to do something consciously, but not actually take action because the power of the subconscious mind overrides our choice. This sets up a potential conflict between the thoughts in the conscious mind and the responses in the subconscious mind. What I was soon going to learn was that when you consciously set out to create something, what you don't know can impede or prevent your success.

Why? We covered this in our seven-minute stick figure presentation, explaining the subconscious mind's characteristics as expressed by Dr. Joseph Murphy, Napoleon Hill, and other proponents of the success philosophy. These characteristics can serve or complicate our conscious efforts.

- The subconscious protects our physical existence and maintains what it has received and accepted from our outer environment.

- The subconscious has no goals of its own, only executing the goals provided from our conscious mind or outside sources.

- Lacking the power of discrimination that the conscious mind possesses, the subconscious accepts ideas that come from others. As ideas become fixed in this part of the mind, they require no conscious assistance. We call them habits or thought paradigms.

- Once established, the subconscious mind never loses focus on ideas, allowing accomplishments and achievements to take root.

This tendency to create paradigms is what causes us to believe it is extremely difficult to control or change habits. Anyone who has ever worked at overcoming a bad habit or addiction is familiar with the feeling contained in a thought paradigm. Until we are aware of the subconscious and how we may collaborate with it, we may feel as if we are at the mercy of the gods, with no control over the circumstances and conditions in our lives.

Having helped us understand these distinctions of the mind, the next portion of Proctor's course was designed to make us aware that when the subconscious has been conditioned to think one way and a new thought is introduced, it will manifest as a terror barrier to block our progress. The term conveys fear, but sometimes it expresses as boredom, giving up, or losing interest because a task feels too hard to accomplish. Once encountered, we express a multitude of excuses as to why we cannot do something, or we deny that we have any part in the problem. And frequently, we retreat back to the starting point to begin all over again. I call it a belief barrier, because paradigms can become the biggest block to achieving our goals if we don't believe something will happen or that it can be done. As Dr. Joseph Murphy put it, "belief trumps desire every time."

Essentially all of our habitual behaviors are on automatic pilot through the subconscious. When we consciously set goals to change a behavior, we also have to change habits and beliefs where they reside in the subconscious mind, or we will fail. Why? Because setting goals is a function of the conscious mind to achieve something new. Goals do not affect the subconscious without additional work.

Habits become beliefs. Personally, it has taken me a long time to grasp that changing these beliefs can be as easy as changing your mind. When I first began to study with Bob, I approached him with what I perceived as a lifetime challenge for me. I had never been able to raise money for movie projects. He called me on it and told me not to say that anymore. Just stop. At the time, I didn't get it at all. How could he say that to me?

It took me a few years of constant study and painful experience before I learned how to "flip my thinking." It really is that simple. The results may or may not be instantaneous, but as your dominant thoughts change, the results follow your dominant thinking. I did not "get it" until I did. Like standing on that trapeze platform, I needed to find a tool that empowered me to change my dominant thoughts. In my case, I learned a questioning technique that created a partnership between my conscious desires and the subconscious mind. In my experience, it is a bit like exercising a muscle. In the beginning, results trickle in, but as the muscle gets stronger, the results improve as well.

Another interesting characteristic of the subconscious is that, other than evaluating whether our ideas match previously defined goals, it does not discriminate or pass judgment on choices or results. It has no sense of past or future. There is only the present—now. The subconscious mind does not judge content, but it moves in the direction of our strongest feelings and dominant thoughts, operating in an orderly manner that is often called "the law." For good or bad, it follows our dominant thoughts, building upon what we have previously thought. If we don't like the results we are getting, then we need to review our thoughts and feelings, because it is the combination of these two components that moves us into action and leads to results. The combination of thoughts, feelings, and actions is what is perceived by others as our attitude.

I'm not saying this is easy to do. It requires vigilant monitoring. I've already described the ways that Peter and I used the power of the conscious mind immediately after the landslide. On the positive side, we knew what we wanted, and our conscious minds were intensely focused on it at all times. We knew our situation and had discerned the positives and negatives in it. We talked together often and searched for the image we had in our minds.

However, fear and negative paradigms were not so easy to wrangle. One of the most challenging things I faced was the fear that permeated the situation. I had to work at keeping my mind closed to any negativity or thoughts of "it cannot be done." There were many nights when I could not sleep and days spent with a vast empty pit in my stomach.

This is where faith came in. To get past the angst, the tossing and turning, I had to have faith in a power greater than myself, as I understood it. And where did I get my faith? Over the years, I had used prayer, meditation, and contemplation to connect to my subconscious mind, and through it, to quantum consciousness, God.

The subconscious mind is our most direct link to our spiritual side, or more scientifically, quantum possibility, limitless except for the limits we consciously choose. Years of study have led to my awareness that the perennial philosophy, ancient wisdom teachings, religions, mystics, and success principles all agree with quantum physics in the understanding that quantum consciousness is a unity, linked to everything else in the universe. We exist within it. As one of its thousand names, it is *that in which we live and move and have our being.*

What does that mean to us? It means that utilizing the subconscious, we can connect to this universal field to receive guidance from within. It may not demonstrate as a genie instantaneously bringing what we desire, but it can provide impressions ranging from feelings of peace and well-being to the quantum leaps of information that physicist Goswami describes as telltale signs of the Divine.

These impressions are highly subjective and anecdotal in nature. Those with a more materialistic point of view may dismiss them entirely in their subtlety. My own experiences are subtle impressions, an insight into situations through focused receptivity in meditation or through physical touch. Others get goose bumps and chills when they experience the connection between something in the outer world with feelings and ideas they have in their inner thoughts.

I have friends who are called "sensitives." Their experiences may be auditory and visual. When I asked, spiritual transformation guide Reverend Barbara Marie (Babish) wrote me how she may become aware of something in her environment in an enhanced way: "I suddenly know it or I see it in more detail... For instance, if I become aware of a flower that is in my home, which has been there for a long time, all of a sudden I see how beautiful it is and I see it in much more detail than ever before. Sometimes I might have a new awareness of something that I thought I already knew. Now, though, it is like I know it at a deeper level."

Or she may be guided. "When I am being guided, it is only with suggestions. For example, if I am being guided by an angel or a guide in my own personal experience, they give me choices. The choices always line up with what I want to accomplish. There is not usually a right or wrong choice. It is usually that one choice will flow in my life better than the other. The actual effect of the guidance is... joy, for me in knowing that I am not alone and that someone cares about what I do and how I do it." Barbara also may receive images.

Another friend and colleague, Genevieve Gerard (guide, speaker, www.genevievegerard.com), wrote me: "When one feels guided, it is a blending of the insight and wisdom of the Soul into the practical aspects of the personality... I have learned over the years to both value and 'listen' to that wisdom. For me, it is most often auditory and is an aspect of Soul contact through meditation. It is best described as a still quiet internal voice. "That said, I do sometimes receive images or what, for want of a better term, could be called visions. For me these are rarer, and when I have received visions it seems to have been because the information and guidance being imparted was more complex so a more 'multi-media' approach was required… As the wisdom imparted in these places and experiences is more focused upon understanding concepts of healing or service, they are less subject to being contaminated by my own personality and emotional or mental constructs so they are in that way more profound, and having received that vision, are a place I can and do return to often for the gifts, wisdom or insight that are there for me. In all revelatory experiences, whether 'the still small voice of Soul' or a dynamic growing and changing vision, it is important that the experience resonate with your inner sense of truth, which in my experience is always clear. Experiences of being guided have always had a profound and often life-changing influence in my life because if I listen or see what I am being directed to, it creates a profound call to action, a call to service."

Receiving guidance of this nature raises another question: Is such guidance always accurate? I polled my friends on this, and the consensus is that guidance is accurate in direct proportion to our willingness to hear the answer.

Barbara Marie wrote: "Yes, I would say it is always accurate, but then my guidance comes as being given choices. I will also say that the very rare times that I do not listen are when I do not like any of the choices I am given. A human reaction to guidance sometimes is this: I ask a question. Who is better for me—the blond man or the brunette man. The answer then comes as choices… If you want a rich man and to be a slave to him, then marry the blond man. If you want an equal partnership, marry the brunette man. *But* I really want to be with a rich man. Who wouldn't? So I disregard the answer that I received and ask a psychic the same question. I keep asking different beings or different people until I get the answer I want to hear. So you see, it is not accurate guidance that I would have been seeking, but seeking the answer I wanted to hear. But back to the main question… I find that the guidance is always accurate."

Likewise, Jenny wrote: "If I am being truthful with myself, that guidance and voice is always right, and is always accurate. That said, it is certainly possible to ignore that voice or try to interpret the information through the lens of my desires, and as such, clutter it with glamour and illusion, so the most significant factor in receiving Soul guidance, Soul wisdom, and Soul insight lies in the ability to be detached and not try to force the guidance into agreeing with what I want to hear or believe." To me, receptivity to these experiences through the subconscious requires faith, and in today's secular society, faith may be weakened or lacking. As Napoleon Hill wrote, "Faith makes it possible to have that which man can conceive and believe." Hill emphasized that developing the power of faith in our daily world was central to achieving our goals. I feel fortunate to have been born with a strong faith, which deepened over the subsequent months after the landslide. However, the wondrous thing is that even people who do not believe in anything at all can still work with the mind to develop faith, and its twin belief, through the persistent "suit up and show up, do the work and be of service" that is incorporated into the creative process. In essence, they may not have faith in an "other-worldly" experience, but they have faith in process. Organizations that utilize sponsors encourage new members to trust that even when we do not understand what is happening, something is going on and will be revealed in its own time. And over and over again, it is.

As we hold a desire in our conscious mind, it is the subconscious that enables us to follow through on the persistent actions that develop the belief required to achieve our goals. If success is the progressive realization of a worthy ideal, belief can be the result of progressive accomplishments in even the smallest increments. Belief is a necessary component. First we see the vision and plan for its achievement; then we gain the knowledge and systems to achieve, and take action. Yet all the pieces can be in place and the actions be taken without kicking over into a higher gear. Why? What stops us? Belief seems to be the missing ingredient.

Have you ever heard that expression, "I'll believe it when I see it?" *Actually, you'll see it when you believe it.* That's because belief in our thoughts creates our reality. The how always comes after the vision, decision, and belief. One way we create these beliefs is by telling ourselves a thought repeatedly until we no longer need to think about it consciously and it becomes a habit.

How did this apply to Peter and me—or to you? After we moved into the new ranch and I began to study with Bob, I thought a great deal about what we were doing that was making huge changes in our situation. First, we knew what we wanted, but mentors told us we also had to know what we were willing to give in return for it. I'm not sure that we consciously knew what we were willing to give, but we worked hard at clearing out the house, saving what we could, caring for our animals, and working through the financial issues. We accepted jobs as they appeared and handled the critical issues around them. I acted on hunches. Some seemed crazy in 20/20 hindsight; however, even one nugget of information could have been valuable, and I was hanging onto all possible solutions. As I became aware of a solution to explore, I did it. I was taking no chances that I might miss an opportunity through my lack of awareness or misinterpretations.

This was about our home; it was the one thing in that moment that we most cared about. We were able to associate our desire for a roof over our head and a long-term space for the entire family with the basic motives of survival. Almost everything was activated: love for our group, financial survival, self-preservation, freedom to live as we liked, expressing ourselves as we desired, anger over the bureaucratic process, and fear of what would happen if we were unsuccessful. There was not a day that went by when we were not critically aware of the benefits we would derive from achieving our definite major purpose; each day we underwent strong emotional feelings about it. And there was not a day when we did not make at least one definite step toward our goal, acting as if we were able to move into our house, until cosmic habitforce kicked in to carry us to the finish line.

We are told that every challenge carries with it the seed of an equivalent value, but it's extremely difficult to accept defeat and setbacks as a testing period and carry on with the belief that it will all work out. But this is exactly what needs to happen. Recently a friend sent a passage: "Sometimes God Says Not Yet." Just because something has not happened yet does not mean that it will not happen at all.

CHAPTER 9

CARE AND FEEDING
OF A DREAM

My daily experience was filled with "not yets." I had a small group of people who valued my insights, but had yet to develop a coaching clientele. The center certainly had not happened yet. It was a fantasy for me.

The center wasn't just a piece of land. It was on a cruise ship or an existing conference locale. It could be a virtual or physical spiritual fitness center, with a variety of activities: body workers leading yoga, tai chi, walking, running, biking, riding through beautiful landscapes, dancing, equine leadership, or kinesiology; and retreat masters guiding centered prayer, meditation, singing, writing, labyrinths, "carry water, chop wood" experiences, gardening, cooking, painting, and studying of success principles, all working as a team in a spirit of cooperation and a sense of accomplishment. The center was a space for vision and guidance toward the next step or action plan. My part was to share the principles and provide access for the work of others.

However, a sharp contrast existed. Evaluating the cost to set up a physical center of this nature, including the cost to run it with housekeeping, administrative staff, gardeners, teachers, yoga instructors, and body workers, I came up with a figure of $600,000 per year, money I did not possess. I've learned that each time I want something that is beyond my ability to make it happen on my own, it's incredibly uncomfortable. The stress is almost physically painful. I want to quit, but know that the consequences of quitting outweigh the discomfort in the long run.

When working with the creative process, getting through the discomfort becomes an investment in faith, without any external signs that a positive outcome is possible. Today when I feel that way, I have the added benefit of Bob Proctor's voice in my head saying, "If you're not living with a little discomfort, you're not standing close enough to the edge… you're living too safely." Stretching out of my comfort zone is now a familiar feeling, one I've had since I began to train as a coach. It's generally accompanied by a certain amount of high drama during the indecision period, but I've also learned that once you make a decision, pro or con, the stress vanishes.

The deliberate creation process is a composite of mental vision, emotional belief, and physical actions. Together, they stimulate results. All three need to be present. You can visualize and beat your head against the wall taking actions, yet get no results unless you have the necessary elements of belief that something can happen. Strong belief enhances the vision and the actions.

Most of what I have described up until this point is largely about those steps. You conceive of an idea that becomes a full-blown vision of something you wish to attain. You gain the required knowledge to be able to execute your vision. You find or develop the system that enables you to take the actions that build your dream, one step at a time, day in and day out, in a consistent, persistent fashion. You are "doing" it. You are busy. You are going through the motions that you have been told will yield the desired results. In fact, all your friends and teachers tell you that you are doing everything right. Keep at it. You have everything you need.

However, this can also be a frustrating time. Why, when you are doing all the right things, can progress stop? A huge question may be looming over your head: Why isn't it working?

Or you might be asking, at what point do we move beyond going through the motions (studying, networking, practicing) to become the manager, publisher, producer, artist, marketer, or author of our dreams? Whatever our vision, what is the trigger that causes a shift from "doing" to "being"? We would all like to have a trigger that could catapult us to the life we have created in our visions. However, the reality is that overnight successes are rare. Our work is to keep going through the action steps we have defined, even if we are only making incremental progress.

This is a very dangerous period in the creative process. Our frustrations are so high and the solution so unclear. We begin to question ourselves. How do we move forward? Should we continue on this path? Do the costs outweigh the benefits? Have we been deluding ourselves? No one else can decide this for us. Ironically this is, in fact, the moment when we need to persist in spite of all the evidence to the contrary. Remember, outer circumstances are not an indication of what is possible. Continuing to take the outer actions we have so diligently identified and practiced will need to continue for at least a couple of reasons. First, it is easier to keep a partially moving flywheel going than to start from a point of non-movement. Second, the power of cosmic habitforce depends on outer work in order to position us to be able to access the inner work we need to do in order to become the results. The trigger is hidden in the inner work.

What I have found for myself is a tendency to get so buried in the details of actions toward goals that the vision itself is lost. When we get trapped in the outer activity, we think we could make better progress if we switched activities. However, if we do that, we lose the traction and momentum of habitforce. Then we would have to repeat it all over again to reach the same point. But there is another solution. While we continue to participate in the habitual activities, we can go back to our internal vision of the desired result and reverse our thinking. The solution may be as simple as looking at what is working and which activities match our desires in order to change the earlier question from "why isn't" to "why is" it working.

Ponder this. What if the believing is the becoming? The achievement mind-set is at once about holding a vision of what we wish to achieve, taking regular persistent actions toward that goal, and becoming that which we wish to be before there are any outer signs in our lives. Much of what we do to create belief is centered on finding ways to keep our vision before us and simultaneously engage in inner and outer processes that help us become the person we want to be. Inner processes are tools and methods such as meditation, affirmations, visualization, yoga, and healing modalities that impact our inner thoughts. They tend to be more intuitive and affect how we feel about something, which then affects what we do. Outer processes are more logical and analytical, like goal planning, time management, effective questioning, journaling, exercise, and skill building.

It's relatively easy to do the outer activities that support becoming. Pop into creative offices, and you'll see signs everywhere that the belief process is at work. Whiteboards are filled with meaningful words, to-do lists, Gantt charts, and drawings. Desktops and tables are littered with models, schedules, scripts, budgets, business plans for investors, and wish lists of talent. Game plans are drawn out. Elaborate scenarios decorate the walls. In the business community, these are recognized components of a successful venture and generally requested before an investment banker will provide venture capital. Everyone realizes that if you fail to plan, you plan to fail. It is a challenge to the beginner, though, who has not yet learned what is required and why it is so valuable to have a mentor or apprentice to someone who has been through the ropes before you.

We want to take our creative process into our private lives, as well as our professional ones, in order to support our belief in the outcome of a dream project. That's why vision boards are so popular. They are visual representations that communicate a dream in tangible form. A written action plan, coupled with a vision board, helps to make the invisible visible. It is common for us to find external ways to support our belief quotient.

We are all familiar with the traditional training venues when major shifts have to happen for someone to learn a new field. Knowledge, especially specialized knowledge, can be purchased or acquired. When we know that we need such information, we rally our resources to begin a course of study or a hiring search. This is not necessarily going to generate immediate results unless you can start right where you are, but people with large visions accept what they can do right this moment and what will take added time to acquire. They build it into their long-term action plan, proceeding to work at segments of the plan over time, holding the overview of the curriculum on their vision board and checking off each course that marks a step toward completion as it occurs. Contrary to popular opinion, this process may contribute more to ultimate success than pure talent. The entertainment industry is filled with many people with talent who never "make it" or become one-show wonders, lacking the discipline to support their talent on a continuous basis.

Whenever possible, plug into existing systems. Reinventing the wheel can require unnecessary time, energy, and money. Organizations that have experience in a given area design systems that can be duplicated by each person who joins the group. The big studios develop paper trails and systems that each crew member and administrative staff incorporate into their daily routines. Self-help groups, like twelve-step programs, suggest that their adherents focus on a process that has demonstrated successful results when practiced faithfully. In a similar vein, marketing organizations create a system that is easy to plug into and easy to duplicate in order to build successful teams. It is one of the advantages that led Robert Kiyosaki to call network marketing the business of the twenty-first century. Each member of the sales organization can focus on core commitments (habitual key performance actions such as two calls per day), proven over time to be effective at obtaining the desired results.

But what happens when you are not aware of such a system, don't fit the circumstances, or resist what others suggest to you? On several occasions, I felt that I lacked such a system. I was operating in blind faith, without a keen sense of exactly what effective actions would be. I thought I knew what I wanted—a system that would enable me to combine my vision and training to build a successful coaching practice. Such a practice was a prerequisite to the center as I envisioned it. I asked for a system, and guidance on systems came to me as intuition and resources that I had never noticed before. As I watched, I was also looking for someone who was successful at building a coaching business.

Who had the qualities that I would like to have in my life? The logic of the old apprenticeships to a master made sense as I sought to build my personal system. Bob Proctor was certainly a good role model, always inspiring us to try something new or something that I would not have tried in other times, but I was not prepared to transplant from our home to apprentice with him.

As I moved through my coaching training, I began to glean something else I hadn't expected. Virtually every program I encountered involved offering a product or service that required getting others to purchase it, whether I was being marketed to or was learning how to market for myself. Proctor himself suggested that his students should write a book.

This rang a bell for me. Peter could use an additional way to raise Caravan West's visibility. We could self-publish a second edition of his first book, and as I returned from a week's training with Bob Proctor, the person we needed to make that happen was sitting in our living room. Kim Barbieri had come to offer her services to Peter. A visual marketer, Kim understood book layouts, websites, and visual marketing. She was familiar with ad sales. The three of us dove into the task of reconstructing the original book, then creating multiple websites. It took a year to accomplish. The second edition was well-received so we decided to publish more books that Peter would author. Another year passed, working, studying, writing, and publishing in our spare time. It was very similar to television and film production, but much more self-contained, and I enjoyed it.

In contrast, in spite of past experience in television and seminar production, my first attempts to garner participants in my own coaching offerings yielded dismal results. Given the economic downturn, Kim and I partnered with another marketer to hold a conference at a local hotel centered on a Bob Proctor theme, "Create Your Own Economy," but no one signed up. I reviewed our work with my mentor Brandon at LifeSuccess, as well as Greg Reid (author, *Three Feet from Gold*). They confirmed that I had done what I needed to do.

I enjoy being a student, but there is a world of difference between the classroom and real life. Stepping out to apply newfound knowledge proved humbling. It was very disappointing. After a Loral Langemeier conference, I started a Blogtalk radio show and garnered a modest audience; however, I had not set it up as a revenue-producing venture. My daily e-mail thoughts fizzled out when the technology had delivery problems. In retrospect, I had not yet learned to differentiate myself. There were so many coaches marketing themselves via the Internet, and I could not answer Loral's question: what kind of a coach was I?

Ted McGrath had taught me that we need vision, knowledge, and a system. I agreed. I needed a system that would attract people to work with me. I knew a variety of ways to organize programs and where to offer them, but I needed to let people know about it. I turned my thoughts to focus on marketing in order to "put butts in the seats."

What's funny is that if you allow it, there is a progression of events that reveal resources just as you focus on a subject. It was true when we blindly recovered from the landslide—and it was true now, as I continued to ask in my prayers and journals for what I perceived to be the missing piece of the puzzle: some element of sales, marketing, and systems that I didn't have.

Ironically, She Who Would Coach Others to success (that would be me) was now overcommitted financially by the pursuit of so many studies. (Although not unusual, it was not terribly comforting to find myself in this situation.) Additionally, it seemed evident that working the long hours and seven-day weeks involved in managing reality television production was not helping me build a coaching clientele.

I constructed a paradigm that if I was to maintain my dream to help others pursue their dreams, I needed to find both a marketing system and regular and residual income with flexible hours. A contrast was activated again. When a contrast is activated by emotionalized thoughts, the subconscious mind is called into action to find a potential solution, even from the most unlikely of sources. In my case, with a few coincidental connections, I fell into the world of network marketing, a form of direct sales. It seemed to match the paradigm I had constructed to maintain my dream.

Just in case you are about to groan, Robert Kiyosaki has written in his book *The Business of the 21ˢᵗ Century* that the network marketing business model is a perfect system to master the basic requirements of a small business. What had I been saying I lacked? A marketing system deconstructed down to its simplest tasks. In fact, as I thought about it, those simple tasks were called key performance actions in the business world. My conscious mind needed to know both what those KPAs were and how they worked in a system that produced the financial results I wanted.

As my subconscious mind would have it, at the first big event I attended, a system was laid out for me via the words of Jeff Olson (author, *The Slight Edge*). In one afternoon, I heard an explanation of a missing piece of the success puzzle that I had been seeking. It was something that I had missed as I studied. Now that we were settled after the landslide, a system of key performance activities, the tasks that have to be performed daily in order to succeed in any given field, eluded me. As I set out in an unfamiliar field, I did not know what they were, nor did I understand their significance.

As I followed Olson's set of action factors, the teaching voices echoed the message: Know the actions that we need to undertake on a consistent basis; persist in spite of what the outer results are showing. These are essential. Doing them is critical.

I listened to motivational coach and speaker Jim Rohn's audios saying that success is relatively simple. It's simple to do. It's simple not to do. Rohn told a wonderful story in his presentations that I came back to repeatedly. It's based on Matthew 13 in the Bible, the parable of the sower. No matter what happened, the sower kept on sowing. The birds came and carried away the seed. Then some seed landed on rocky soil and could not take root. Then some landed among the thorns, which choked off its growth. Still other seed mixed with weeds, and some of the plants yielded only a small percentage of their possible crop. But the sower never let any of these obstacles bother him. He was intent on only one thing—to keep on sowing. He did not let the lack of results stop him from the task at hand, and he received good yield from his fields.

That story is such a perfect success instruction: persist in the face of adversity. There is nothing exciting about sowing seed. In fact, it is a pretty mundane, repetitive action. That is both its strength and its weakness. What is even more amazing is that the act of sowing the seed is not about the quantity of seed sown, but rather that it *is* sown. This was the point that I had missed in all my training—keep sowing the seed, two a day until it builds, five to six actions per day that move you toward your goal. I had heard the word *persistence*, but missed the mind picture.

As I reviewed what I had heard from others, it became clear that the message rang throughout. Build habits that support you to achieve your goals. Do this through your core commitments to specific actions and time management. This is not an instantaneous process. It involves developing your internal mental processor to keep making choices that lead step-by-step to a goal. Twelve-steppers say, "Keep coming back. It works if you work it." It works if you work *with* it is the easier path. Statistics show that 70 percent won't do it. They will listen, but they won't be coachable. They won't risk the strong currents of desire. Instead, they will make excuses or blame others and the company they work for if they are unsuccessful.

That applies to us too. By repeatedly choosing to do certain simple daily and regular tasks, thinking the same thought or repeating the same words over and over again, we build habits that will sustain us as we move forward. This foundation is part of what Napoleon Hill calls the third essential step in developing the persistence we will need to keep working toward our goals in spite of all the detractors, excuses, distractions, harsh conditions, and unknown periods of gestation that will be required. These habits provide the basis of activity that enables us to keep on keeping on, closing out all negativity and overcoming all doubts while going through the process.

They also do something else. They begin to generate the energy that supports us and takes over once we have established the power of habit. Involved in daily television production as I have been, I feel this energy when it becomes a comfortable routine in which all the activities flow together. It is the energy of a flywheel, which keeps turning with little effort once established. The challenge is to start the flywheel turning. It can be so difficult to move the wheel that everyone would give up without faith and belief, the essential ingredients to our stick-to-itiveness.

People don't always like to hear that they create their own reality, but can you see how you can do that by choosing to allow the establishment of bad habits? Once the habit is in place, we feel powerless over it. By that point, we are dictating our own limitations through the thoughts we're holding in our minds. It's as if we have put up a wall through which consciousness cannot penetrate until we remove the restrictions. If we allow the expression, pure consciousness flows. If we resist, it cannot. The image we hold in our minds dictates the limits that are placed on power as it flows to and through you.

For me, that translated into what is a common experience. Once we have a vision in place, we set out to get it. Somewhere in our conditioning, we hold a belief that we control outcomes through our own activities. When we do not see results, we may start to cast about for something we can do about it. It may lead to busywork or to targeted actions that underscore our goals. It seems crazy to just wait, holding an image of what we want. We want to know how everything is going to happen and are delighted when someone offers us what might be called tricks of the trade. We would be delighted if the answer were as simple as tithing each week or learning to keep a daily planner, both of which can be valuable tools to help us.

I worked with one of those daily planners designed to refocus my efforts toward my long-term goals every day. As usual, the process starts with the big vision, this time expressed as a five-year vision plan. However, because few people can hold the "big picture" continually, either getting distracted or blinded to the steps we need to take, this planner asked us to break our goals down to sizes that we can handle in a short period of time. What needs to be accomplished in one year in order to move forward in the next?

Target goals are broken down and entered into monthly, weekly, and daily goals, then daily phone calls, meetings, and appointments. These daily actions have the virtue of building up consistent activity that kicks in the power of cosmic habitforce, increasing our belief level, as well as creating a layer of accountability, if only to ourselves. The key is to focus on one specific target at the level we can handle until we are successful, regardless of what deadline we choose.

(Deadlines are usually recommended, but they can be tricky. They can be the source of procrastination if you wait for the approaching date before beginning to take action. Or as the date approaches with no sign of the desired results, you may lose faith, feel intensified angst if the date passes, or have a sense of looming failure. If you are prone to "head trash" when deadlines approach, you may want to focus on accomplishments from a "milestone map" rather than specific dates. I'll talk about that shortly.)

Just keeping the calendar may lead us to believe we are doing the work, but we have to take actions related to those goals and maintain them. Surrounding ourselves with others who have been successful in the same arena may help, because they already know the specific tasks that lead to the fastest results. In television, we know the daily tasks that need to be accomplished in order to meet our production schedules. (We also have a great sense of urgency. Failure is not an option.) In network marketing, managers or sponsors train us to make routine calls, book appointments, do presentations, invite people to events, participate in a number of core commitments, understand a game plan, and work with our new team members to help them do the same things. These are not extravagant goals. Experience demonstrates that routine activities need to be simple to do or people will not keep doing them.

From my personal experience, it is not enough to just dream and create castles in the air, any more than it is enough to just go through the motions of daily activity. Quantum physics has demonstrated that the creative process has four stages. In the first, it's our conscious job to start the process by identifying and focusing on a vision without getting buried in the details of the game plan and specific actions. It's not that we're not pulling together a string of consistent activities. In fact, regular actions come together to produce the desired results. However, the subtle difference between taking actions and being swamped by them is extremely important. The next two stages, unconscious processing and rapid collapse from quantum consciousness to the tangible world, take place on the nonconscious level. That is where the subconscious takes care of the how. Finally, the fourth stage occurs after the subconscious has completed its work. It usually appears as an insight, intuition, or quantum leap, after which positive work can be accomplished. We can then monitor the results for any contrasts between the original vision and what we received.

To be honest, as I started to learn about consistent activity in network marketing, I knew very little about the network marketing environment. I wanted to do well, so I set out to learn how I could attain recognizable results each month. I was focused on doing everything my sponsor and trainers told me to do. I attended two meetings each week. The corporate office arranged qualifying courses in the various product lines. I took each one. I wrote a five-year plan for my calendar and envisioned it already fulfilled. My days were focused on one goal at a time. I planned results, writing out lists daily—the to-do list and ideas for the next day. I studiously worked at catching and correcting behaviors that did not support my efforts.

At times, I felt as if I were in a laboratory, experimenting with the power of visualization. Corporate sales management expected us to attend conventions two to three times per year in distant locations. With my finances dwindling, getting to each convention felt like a miracle of manifestation; one literally fell into place twenty-four hours before I had to be on a flight to South Carolina.

That particular story is a good, isolated example of the manifestation process. For me, it begins with "dwelling" on a given situation. I had a little cash available from a holiday gift Peter had just given me, but I had very little belief that I could go on this trip. We are taught that if we do not believe in a thing, we will not take the required actions to make it happen, so in order to overcome my lack of belief, I began taking actions that demonstrated belief.

What I ultimately did echoes a story that Dr. Joseph Murphy included in his book *The Power of Your Subconscious Mind*. When you want to take a trip and do not have a penny in your pocket, believe you have received an answer and then take some action to indicate your faith that your prayer has already been answered. In that story, the person made sure his passport was up-to-date, packed a suitcase with everything needed for the trip, and put it at the door ready to go. He then imagined his arrival at his destination until he received an impression that something was actually happening. The instructions were augmented by suggesting that he stay in the present, expecting something wonderful and speaking with the subconscious as he would speak to a friend. In the end, he received the resources he needed and made the trip.

Wayne Dyer also contributed to my thought process when I caught one of his programs on PBS. Dyer stated that in any given situation, either a positive or a negative result could be possible. Since we cannot predict which result will arrive, focus on the positive. It was just the suggestion I needed as I struggled with expectation.

For me, the positive result would be going to South Carolina, so I turned my wholehearted attention to the trip. In the weeks just prior to the anticipated convention, I had been distracted by plans for holidays, shopping, wrapping and shipping presents. Once they were done, I could focus on the task at hand. I began by prayerfully watching for every opportunity to present itself. I wrote affirmation statements that what I desired was already happening. Affirmations have always worked better for me when I have a very short-term, targeted goal. Fortunately for this trip, the time line was quite short. I knew exactly what had to be done. I created a to-do list every day.

Then I began to evaluate the tasks I would be undertaking if I were preparing for a trip like this. I began to do each of those tasks, short of actually spending the money I did not possess. I began to watch for the best air travel deals. I reconfirmed my possible housing arrangements in the area. I did the laundry and began packing, even though there was no evidence that I would be going anywhere. It would have been easy to give up and not think about it anymore; I did not have enough money to make that trip. Instead, I chose to stay open and willing. I continued to search for a way. I defined how much money I would need in order for me to go, as well as the maximum air ticket price.

Since your conscious mind can get in the way of the results you desire when you are emotionally distressed, Dr. Murphy wrote that the best thing you can do is to let go, relax, and still your thoughts. In fact, the subconscious mind works better when the conscious mind is quiet. Therefore, he suggested we turn over a specific request to the subconscious just prior to sleep.

Once I had the idea in mind, had done what I could to be ready when things came together, and had a list of ongoing items that remained undone, then it was time to turn it over to my higher power. Let go and let God. I had to be willing to accept that it might not happen—and that it was also possible that it could happen. I had to be willing to take action when the moment was right, so I kept monitoring the situation.

At the very last minute, all the pieces came together—Priceline had a flight and car at a low price, one of my associates had an event ticket and room in her hotel room, laundry was done, packing and errands were quickly run, new associates signed up, and I found myself sitting on the plane heading for South Carolina. If I had given up, the new sales revenue might have arrived; however, I would not have had all the other components lined up, ready to go. It is possible that I could still have pulled it all together with a great deal of last-minute effort; however, there was no need to find out.

Seeing how the deliberate creation process worked, I was clearly enthusiastic about working with it again. I wanted to be a role model for my sales team. Returning from South Carolina, I was supercharged. I quickly earned the requisite points for sales activity and earned my position in their Performance Club. Imagine my disappointment when I couldn't recreate the sales activities to get into it again the next month… or the next…

One year later, my personal finances were woefully insufficient. I was depending on Peter for everything, and because we had never run our lives that way, it was very uncomfortable on the home front. His support for my new ventures was rapidly eroding, but it certainly gave me the necessary motivation to kick into a higher gear. Everything I wanted was on the other side of my financial worries. I was barely scraping together enough money to put into my gas tank, let alone anything that I might desire. My plan to use network marketing as a source of regular and residual income was taking too long to satisfy my needs. Additionally, it did not appear to be helping me build either my coaching practice or any kind of center. It was clear that I needed to shift something. Where was I going to go from here?

CHAPTER 10

WHEN IT'S NOT WORKING, PERSIST AND REEVALUATE

Can anything be more disheartening than the period after you have diligently been doing everything you thought necessary, following all the suggested instructions, and participating in all the activities that promise to yield the results you desire—and before you actually see those results? I lacked the perspective to see that I was learning something new, while Peter, whose activities were in high gear, was continuing to build on his lifework. The ranch might appear new; however, it was growing out of everything he had done before. His success only underscored my frustrations.

The reality is that some things just take time. That is the law of gestation. Sometimes we need the patience to allow ourselves to go through this period, remembering that it isn't working *yet*. During that time, the best solution of all is to keep on doing what we have set up as our daily routine and personal habitforce garnered from wiser heads than our own. Staying in effective activity is one of the most powerful choices we can make.

However, there came a point when I wanted nothing more than to quit. Negative emotions flew in the face of my efforts. Overwhelmed by sensations of despair, frustration, guilt, fear, and doubt, all I wanted was relief. I asked myself if it would be better if I gave up. The subconscious resonating with my negative thinking kicked in, screaming warning signs: Danger, Danger! Stop! Go back!

By this point, the changes I had made had taken me outside the entertainment industry. I still wanted to guide; however, because network marketing had the potential to be an immediate, primary source of income, I was devoting the same amount of time in the same way as production. You would have seen me at weekly trainings and briefings, monthly Saturday gatherings, conventions, team and accountability calls. I adored my workout partner. I took special trainings. I read my daily readings in personal development. I created a follow-up box and worked it religiously. I met with many people, but the financial results were barely visible. It wasn't awful. I had a growing team, but no income. I thought I was doing what I was told were the right things; however, no checks were coming in for my efforts.

And I was loath to give up. I firmly believed that the pieces of marketing and discipline I was learning were significant components of my future success and that they would be of great value for my long-term vision.

Ironically, in the midst of this economic downturn, I was surrounded by high-income earners in success coaching who subscribed to the same philosophies: Gerry Robert, Marilyn Jenett, and Mary Morrissey. Their success was directly connected to the basic concepts of the creative or success process. I went through their home-study programs for success, achievement, and manifestation, but as my funds dried up, it became harder and harder to continue in their programs. There were earnings leaders in the network marketing industry: Jeff Olson, Mark Smith, and tens of team leaders. But my financial reality was intractable. Six-figure earners were the guest speakers at the network marketing training events and led my sales team. I understood the law of gestation. I appreciated the Greg Reid book *Three Feet from Gold* and resolved that I would hang in there. I had so many teachers available to me that I could have spent the entire day on calls with them—and that seemed to make no sense at all.

When we operate from sensory experiences and the conditioning that we have received our whole lives from the outer world, we are subject to the ups and downs of an emotional roller coaster, making it extremely difficult to think through our ideas and desires while we feel that way. I now jokingly call this period "Desperately Seeking Successful Susan." It was incredibly confusing. I dropped back to reassess what was going on. I have to admit I was glad to have an arsenal of exercises in my life tool kit to help me manage my emotions at this point, because the feelings that were running riot in my experience threatened to overwhelm me. I'm not the best client by myself. I gain the most when I have someone to help me gain clarity and focus as I talk through the contrasts I am experiencing.

My immediate outer focus was to get cash flowing in order to provide the resources to meet my financial obligations. No one I knew was going to give two hoots about my dream work, and to be quite honest, at this point, I was more concerned about having gas in the tank and food on the table myself. So this became my focus. I kept up my marketing activities; however, I was watching for any work that yielded "time for money" cash flow. I was so desperate to get my finances back on track that as soon as I found a promising opportunity, I set myself to study for and pass a state insurance exam, barely related to any of my stated goals or plans.

As I celebrated passing the exam, the importance of laser-focused activity caught my attention. I was focused when I found the resources needed to travel, to pass exams, to pull the personnel and resources together to build a production "city" for a shoot, and to complete study programs over extended time periods. Peter and I were focused when we were getting through the entire landslide. It struck me that each of these items was a targeted event. They were short-term activities with definite deadlines and consequences. I questioned myself. How could I capture the intensity and focus to get back on my feet financially, as well as gain the resources to consciously achieve a vision when it was more long-term? How would I be able to transfer short-term focus to my longer-term goals? I thought back to what John Assaraf had written. The conscious mind only works in extremely small spurts. It loses focus every six to ten seconds. I use my conscious mind all the time to lay out my goals and to evaluate the results. But just because my conscious mind decides to do something doesn't necessarily mean that it will get done. I can plan, evaluate options, concentrate on all the details of a project, fill out the calendar pages, and make to-do lists all day; however, if I do not engage my nonverbal, nonlinear subconscious mind, nothing will happen. What was the key to getting that 87 percent of my mind on board with my desire to help others? What was stopping me? In my linear life, I stepped back to repeat the process from the beginning once again. Surely I had learned something from the experience of the landslide and all my subsequent training. I started by clearing away that which no longer served me. This ranged from tossing out study materials to straightening spaces in my outer world. Bob Proctor told a great story in his book *You Were Born Rich* about his aunt throwing out old furniture in order to make room for the new. Such activities have everything to do with the vacuum law of prosperity.

Nature abhors a vacuum. As you clear out the old, you make room for the good you desire to flood in to fill the empty space.

As I cleared away the past, I was pondering my vision, reviewing where I was and the contrasts I was experiencing, and taking inventory again.

Where was I? After working for years on production teams, I was now a trained coach and LifeSuccess Consultant working a plan to have a client base sufficient to earn an income and ultimately lead to the retreat and conference center. The contrast between the time demands of production and building this client base had led me to believe that it would not be possible to do both. So I asked for a solution. I had been told that a flextime network marketing business could give me the time and money freedom to make appointments and meet clients as long as I chose, along with the added benefit of residual income.

However, I was caught in a larger contrast. My efforts to market had not gone well. My savings were drained. To compensate, I was spending every working moment doing tasks related to marketing and was not building any clientele. Whatever the conscious plan I had hatched so far, it was not working very well, and Peter was not happy with me.

What was making progress was this book. I started working on it while Peter and I were completing several of his titles. An advertising e-mail from Peggy McColl inspired me to begin to write in earnest, so I pulled out my outline and started to write. The early chapters came together easily; however, as I moved further along, I began to run into blocks. Each time, life experiences and resources would surface to help me explain and craft the next chapter. I was explaining the creative principles to others as I came to understand them from the inside out. One of the most important concepts I was learning was about focus.

Jeff Olson (author, *The Slight Edge*) had emphasized that ultimately our ideas had to be expressed in small, easy actions, whether they were two calls per day or two hours of study for an exam, or we wouldn't do them. Convinced as I was that this was the missing piece of the puzzle for me, I had buried myself in the smaller actions and lost sight of the bigger vision. It was time to get out of the weeds and work at both the actions and the vision simultaneously.

What did I need to do to focus on the big vision as well as the small actions that would take me there? The mental work we do at this stage is to focus, "follow one course until successful" as we allow our dreams to unfold. This requires faith, belief, and an attitude of gratitude, as well as the ability to persist mentally even when physically inactive. Since that flies in the face of our conscious mind's belief that only measurable action in the physical world succeeds, I used a variety of tools to maintain inner activity, while still relaxing and letting go on the physical plane.

No matter the chaos and outward failure around me, the word *book* stood on my whiteboard. When I closed my marketing office for the day, I picked up my research or got on the computer to move it forward.

About this time, another e-mail gave me an idea that tied into the action plans I had studied. The idea was to create a milestone map. A milestone map places all of the major milestones required to achieve a given project into a progressive time line. We may not know all the steps when we sit down to design it, so it may take some time to research even the broad strokes that will be required. The details will be revealed later. The goal in the planning phase is to find out the stages and components involved and when they occur, so that we can lay them out as a map—a milestone map. I liked this idea. It seemed like fun. I would have to do some research, but once I did it, I could design a milestone map to write, publish, and promote this book. When I was ready to sketch it out, the playful aspect rang true for me. As you can see below, I turned mine into a game-board design.

The map revealed something else. Even as I poured my energies into these pages, I recognized that it was only one step on my milestone map. Other milestones emerged in addition to the writing. As I moved around the map, I had milestones for sharing the creative process that could help others experience more joy and improve their lives. More writing, publishing, and collaborating with others to produce their projects could get this information out in ways that would benefit the largest number of people possible. The center could support these creative activities.

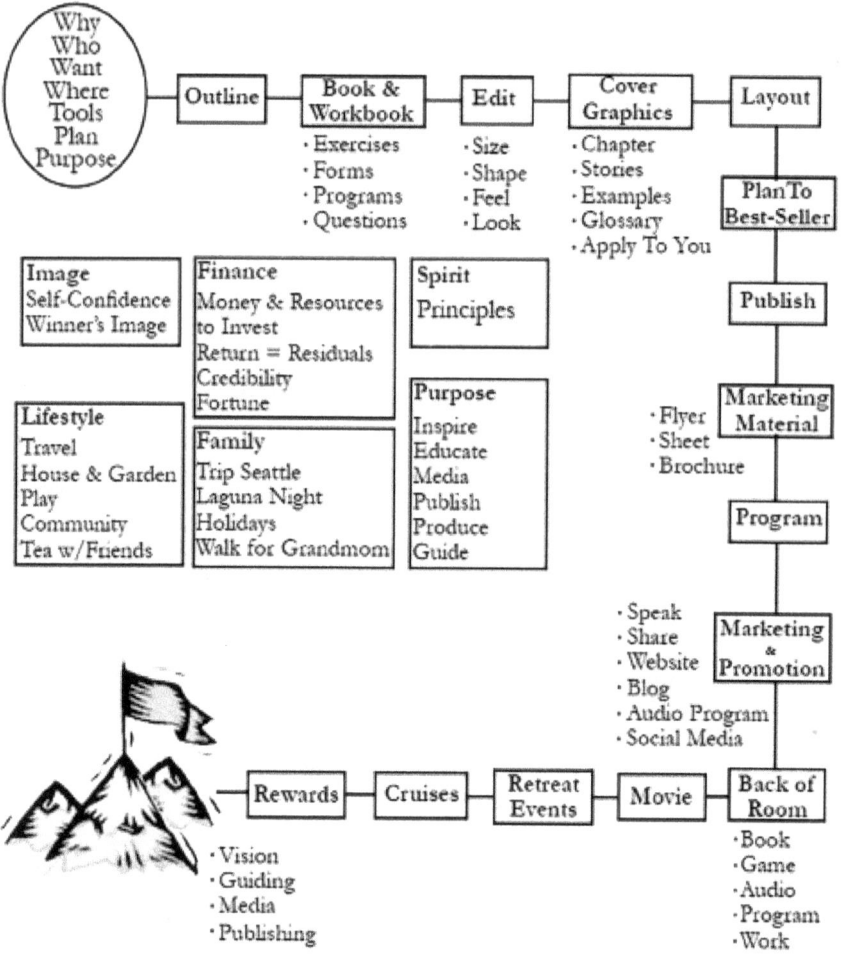

Example of a Milestone Map.>>

As I sought to define my ideas in greater detail, I considered what would have to happen for them to become real. I still had several obstacles to overcome. Seeing castles in the air alone would not do it. I needed to break the steps down into bite-size actions.

The milestone map I created served as a navigation chart. I made a few copies of it, one to tack onto a whiteboard and another to tuck into a notebook where I might stumble upon it from time to time. I did the same thing with index and business cards that contained useful mental jogs. They served as small visual cues that the conscious mind barely noticed until I focused on them; however, the subconscious mind resonated with them in the background through the emotional connection between the image and my goal. It was all part of supervising the execution of a plan.

I also put up mind maps. We can mind map in a variety of formats. In one format, we create concentric circles. In the center circle, we write down one of our goals. A larger circle surrounds the center, divided into the major categories that need to be addressed in order for us to accomplish the larger goal. Then an additional circle surrounds the categories, which are then divided into more specific actions extending out, like spokes in a wheel, from each circle. These items can be used to create daily action lists that support the milestone map we will be following. Progressive goal wheels on my whiteboard helped me keep track of my score. I cut out several circles. In the center, I drew a smaller circle and wrote one of the goals I wanted to attain. I then drew lines from the inner circle to the outer edge. The one I created below was to monitor decreasing weight goals using the spaces between the lines to delineate a starting weight and where I wanted to be. Upon achieving each weight goal, the space was to be commemorated with a gold star or colored with a marker.

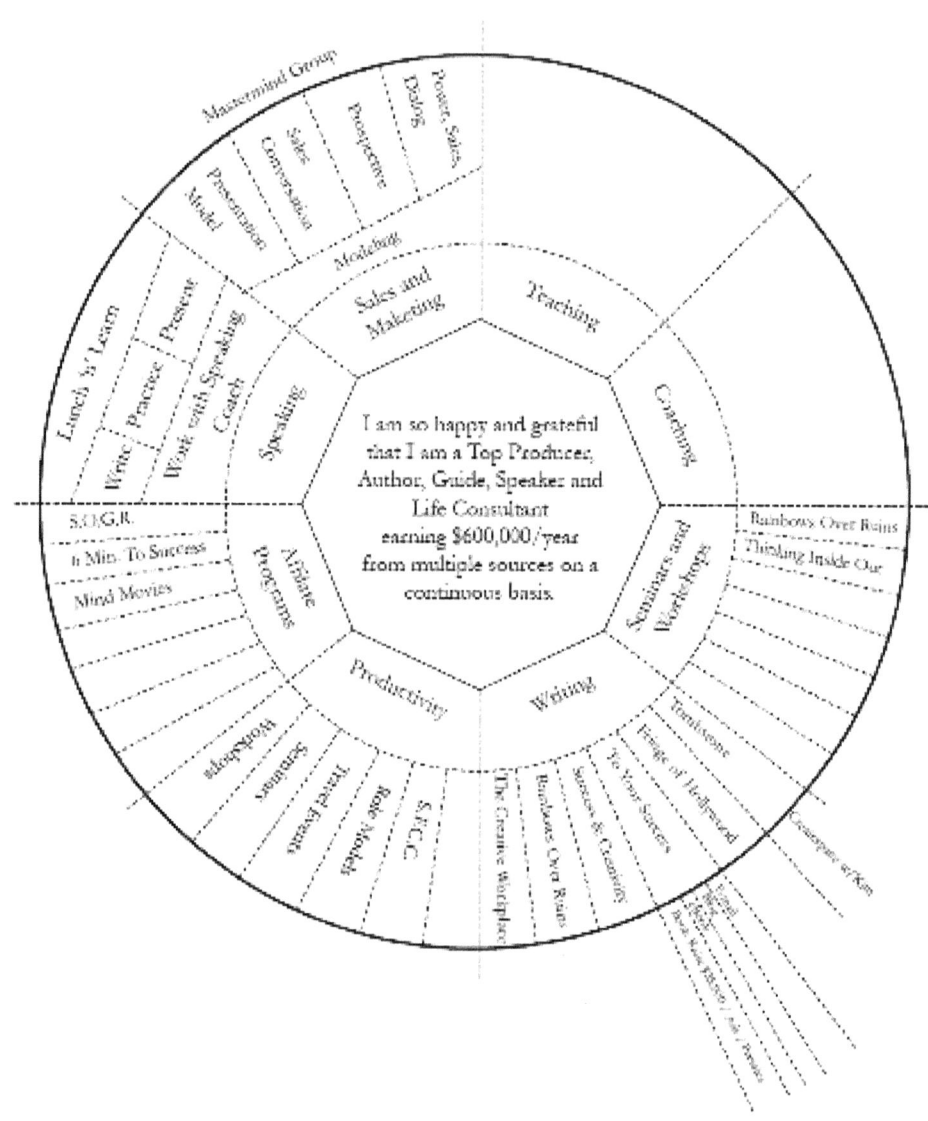

Spoked Circle Diagram

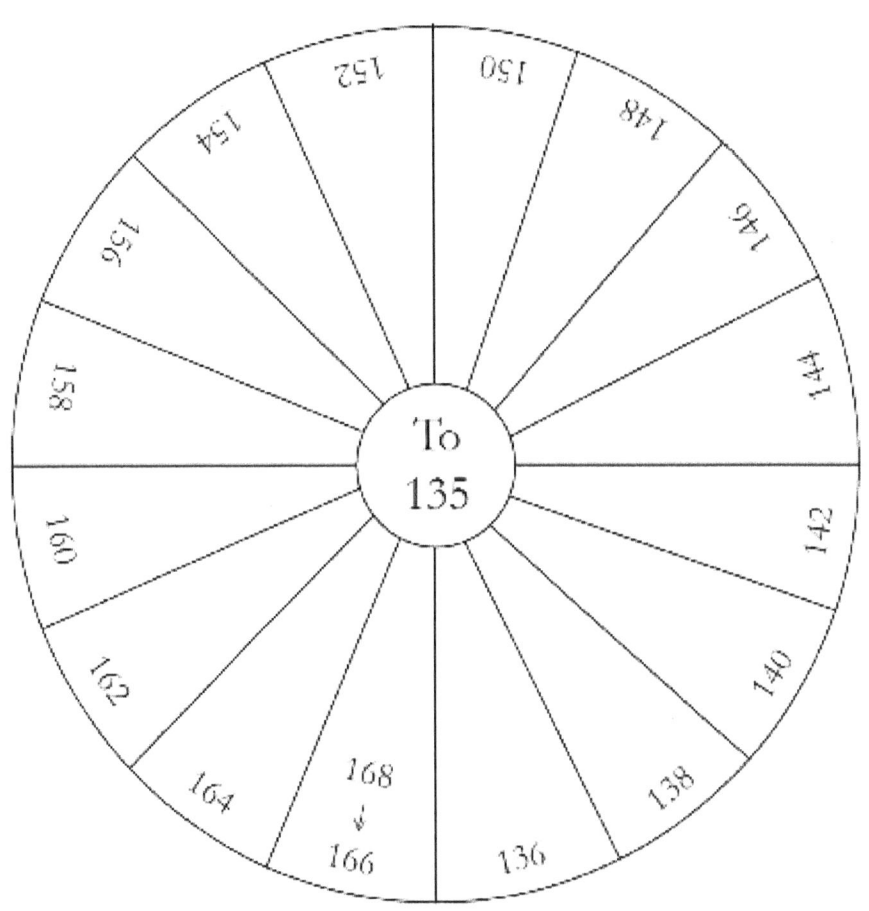

Weight circle

Although the creative process involves inner work, outer activities and visual cues help us maintain our primary goal as our dominant thought.

Over the previous months, I had found myself concentrating on everything I could read and apply about the subconscious. I had learned that our ability to hold a vision is generated by our will, which serves as the director in our life's play. The subconscious stands behind the will, serving the function of supervisor, watching the development of a plan, calling us into action, and providing definite instructions to help us achieve any goal. It helps us to stay on course, subordinating some of the various means we might choose when called upon to adapt in the face of changing conditions and circumstances. It also tells us when to let go and allow the plan to unfold.

The literature emphasized the role of the subconscious as a powerful force to help us survive, along with traditional techniques used to help us get past our own mental roadblocks. It mentioned affirmations or autosuggestions from the conscious mind to the subconscious in order to make changes we desire. It talked about consciously building up new habits, surrounding ourselves with visual cues, and ways to watch and listen for clues that the subconscious is responding.

I had built all of this into my regular activities, but still hadn't seen the progress I expected. I couldn't help wondering if there were reasons for that. I found out that there are many ways in which our undisciplined thinking gets in the way of our success—through ambivalence, resistance, hanging on too tightly, being distracted or unfocused, wearing the blinders of our own opinions even when help is offered, and the stinking thinking of paradigms that surround the conditions, circumstances, and excuses that we toss out to the world.

As I researched the various ways the conscious mind could get in the way of the work of the subconscious, I recognized several in my own thinking. I was often ambivalent, wanting more than one thing at the same time. As I thought about my own situation, it became apparent that I had several conflicting desires. Dr. Murphy had written, "Your subconscious mind cannot act if your mind is divided." I began to consider which of the contrasts I was experiencing was dominant and whether I could resolve the ambivalence.

I'd worked in the entertainment industry through my entire adult life. I now had a strong desire to build upon my avocation to guide others in the pursuit of their dreams by sharing my experience of the deliberate creative process. If we can express what we want or where we want to go, we can develop the way to get there. It wasn't until the landslide that I was given a path to do both as part of my purpose.

The surprise for me was that the persistent, consistent activity necessary to achieve my dream expressed in writing, researching, and publishing books. I might have needed an income, but writing helped me feel more of what I wanted to feel as a guide. Since I was not generating income yet during the writing process, the choice to write rather than call for sales appointments, or even production gigs, ultimately put me in a precarious financial situation. The explanation given in the literature was that without clear, directed, conscious thought, the subconscious seeks clarity at another level, generally through the most strongly felt emotional state of mind or survival instinct, and then acts accordingly. That could also explain something else. I frequently gave myself permission to pursue courses of study and new life experiences like coaching when all was well with my family. However, if they became upset by these studies or experienced financial hardship as a "side stream" effect of my activities, I would stop. Love is such a powerful emotion that it sends a strong message to the subconscious; ergo, I experience an inner conflict under these circumstances. Since all of my efforts had not been working, it made sense that my first priority might have been to ensure the well-being of my family. Perhaps I could resolve the ambivalence by getting honest with myself about my priorities.

My studies were revealing more and more ways that we can interfere with the creative process. I learned about "praying in two directions," which happens when we condemn others who are more successful or more prosperous than we are. We lose what we criticize, so it chases away the very things we are praying to receive. We cannot have it both ways. When praying in two directions, the dominant emotion, especially if one of survival, will dominate the subconscious response.

We may not realize how other people affect us either. Many of the suggestions people make, whether they know it or not, are aimed at making us think, feel, and act in ways that are to their advantage, even if they are destructive to us. Expectations from our family, friends, and peers, especially when we are starting something new, may not support us. Part of what we are striving to learn is to exercise the power to choose what is best for the good of all concerned and to forgive others for not understanding. In the above situations, we may feel powerless to overcome a situation.

The list goes on. We may let our mind chatter ramble without paying much attention to what we are saying or how repetitive some thoughts have become. Do you hear yourself saying that, "there is not enough time or money," "I can't afford that," or "I will not be able to…"? Saying "I can't" and similar phrases can neutralize our prayers, as can using affirmations if we experience an untruth in the stating.

And we can't forget all those negative paradigms that control us. Fortunately, there are ways to overcome them. "Out with the old, in with the new" is the essence of popping paradigms or stating affirmations. We use what we experience as negatives (called contrasts) as clues to what has to change in our thinking. We can then apply tried-and-true techniques such as writing, affirmations, and progressive beliefs to flip our thoughts to support our desired outcomes. Students of the subconscious have determined there are work-arounds to replace all thoughts that stop us with new thoughts that work to our advantage, thus propelling us toward our desires.

So, what are our options when we feel we have created a destructive situation? I felt I needed to fall back and rethink what I was doing. I don't mean that I was giving up, but rather that I was reprioritizing the best way to achieve my dreams. You might think "scrambling" was a better word. I found myself scrambling to achieve the humblest income, to think in the face of family pressure, to make the best choices to get on firm ground again, almost rifling through the variety of tools that could help me face this situation and restore inner calm.

Wouldn't you think that a coach should be able to handle this on his or her own? No, it's not necessarily so. It's very hard to get the perspective you need when you are in the middle of a crisis. Vivian King (with a nod to Einstein) used to remind us that it is impossible to solve a problem at the same level as where the problem exists. We have to get above it. We use therapists, counselors, coaches, and friends to help us gain perspective on the issues. The option I chose in that moment— lacking the capital to call for help—was to draw upon the resources I had been given as I went through my coaching training.

The place to start, they had told me, was to manage my emotions. Wayne Dyer tells us that when you change the way you look at things, the things you look at change. Thus, my goal was to change my perspective of the situation. It is common practice in the self-help field to ask clients to avoid dwelling on the negative aspects of their lives. Too much negative thinking serves to create a movie of what we do not want that will replay later. However, there is some value in acknowledging that there is a contrast between where you are and where you want to be. This pondering of contrasts and thinking through possible actions one may take to resolve the contrast is something Dr. Heidi Grant Halvorsen (author, *Succeed: How We Can Reach Our Goals*) calls "mental contrasting" and "if then" planning. It involves indulging in possibility thinking, complete with affirmations, as well as dwelling on the potential obstacles. The swing between them is the mental contrast. She calls the result "realistic optimism." When it is completed, we should emerge with a clear answer to the question "Is it worth it?" Some of this work may be done in preliminary stages or as a review. What if you are not seeing the results you wanted? Then mental contrasting becomes part of a healthy system to evaluate your choices and determine if it is ever good to give up.

I remember when I first heard Ted McGrath use the question "What's stopping you?" followed immediately by "Step into it." It sounded so simple then. After all, I was in the early stages of living my new life. It was all theory and academics. It felt as if I were at the edge of the known world. For me, saying the words and living them seemed miles apart. I heard the phrase from each teacher: "All you have to do is change your thought-life and keep it changed. Let your habitual thinking be: 'Success is mine...'" The thoughts echoed in my head with little effect. I was beside myself.

So what could be stopping me? I was certainly no stranger to the impact of negative emotions, especially fear. Had I not struggled against its corrosive effect in the immediate aftermath of the landslide? But now, Dr. Murphy's words were in front of me. "When fear knocks at the door of your mind, or when worry, anxiety and doubt cross your mind, behold your vision, your goal." In other words, focus on and get engrossed in a more positive desire in order to release the power of the subconscious, which will then flow in response to your thoughts.

I recommitted to the inner process, asking questions. Did I have blocks? Was I caught up in old paradigms that no longer served? Had I found a point of ambivalence that stopped me cold? I began to see that "asking" has been a huge part of my journey. In my morning writings, I asked my subconscious and "power team" to work from the big picture visions to something immediately tangible. What could I do right now—where I was—to get back on track?

You may be aware of the Biblical story in which Jesus tells his followers, "Ask and it is given." As a coach, I generally receive hundreds of e-mails from other coaches pitching their programs regularly, but my e-mailbox was now filled with messages from people asking questions. I found myself responding to some questions and asking others. While watching and listening for the answers, "how" to ask took on a new importance, and changes began to occur very rapidly.

I had been taught that questions asked when in a state of appreciation release the power of the subconscious to line up resources and individuals that begin to surface in your life to help you. However, sometimes we are so focused on the exact way we picture the way forward that we may miss the help when it appears. That's why Dr. Joseph Murphy instructed all to watch—your thoughts, who or what comes into your space—and pray.

So to achieve the receptive state created by appreciation, I continued to start my daily meditation by counting my blessings, expressing gratitude for the joys I had in my life, as well as anything that occurred that aligned with my desires. Then I began to follow the instruction to let go and trust the nonconscious power greater than my conscious mind, source, to provide the means to receive my needs. I attempted to let go of any preconceived ideas of how that would show up and prayed for Divine guidance.

Somewhere in the middle of all the chaos and discomfort, I could feel a sense of inevitability. My dream called to be birthed. The book called to be written, the activity had become habit, those around me were supporting me to the best of their ability (even if they were yelling and screaming at me), and I kept at it, pushing at the flywheel, thanks to the support of habits I'd established. I was in the water, sink or swim. I had to do what I had to do. I had the strength to persist, mouthing the words, "I will until…" even in the face of all these difficulties, even though I was "stuck."

Being stuck feels physical. You feel it even if you don't recognize it for a while. Then suddenly you begin to use the words, "I'm stuck. I can't seem to move forward. I'm doing everything, but it's not working." When you can name it, you can claim it and tame it. Being able to see that you are stuck is the first step in getting unstuck. Being stuck has its physical solutions. It works if you work it. Keep on keeping on. But there is also inner work that needs to be done to get unstuck.

At these moments, it would be great if we could hear the bugler's call and know that the cavalry was on its way to rescue us. Isn't that the way it always happens in Westerns? But real life is not structured like a movie. Rather, it is often best lived by connection to the life force that we see evidenced around us. For me, it is the experience of returning to the still, centered space of my existence.

What began to happen next occurred rapidly but without the experience of haste. For that reason, I have included dates to help you get a sense of the time frame.

Around March 18, I asked a question about ambivalence. In my journal that day, I described how I saw the process as a puzzle. We start with a vision (the box cover) and a huge pile of pieces that we have to sort by color or outside edges to find the like-minded pieces that fit. Then we keep trying to figure out how they all fit together. Sometimes it's really boring and tedious. I sensed this was an answer to one of my questions: focus on one puzzle at a time, allowing the various colors to fit where they do.

By March 23, a question came to me during journaling. "Why am I doing what I do?" I responded: to help others activate the power of possibility, to provide a vehicle for them to do so, to dream and then to see that these do not have to be wishes and idle dreams. They can attract them by their thoughts and daily choices of actions.

And the question came, "What do you want?" As we express our desire, we ask and we hold the thought. Sometimes we are so busy holding the vision and sending out affirmations, as well as asking and describing what is not quite right yet, that we take back the "how" from our higher power. We behave as if we have to do everything.

"May we suggest that you choose instead to describe what you would prefer, and we (source life force) will define and create the adjustments? So, what is the contrast you are experiencing?" I have immersed myself in an MLM in order to learn the application of thought to effective action on a consistent, persistent basis. The results are modest. We are pulling from assets in order to continue. I would prefer a *new* flow—meaning flow from coaching, creating my MLM, publishing, speaking—rather than what feels like depleting assets. Think of it as transferring that which no longer serves… of moving one form of stagnant energy to a new and higher use. Clear up, box up, and sort. Is that effective action?

"Are you buying someone else's lifestyle?" But…

"Relax. When do you feel the best?" When I am creating. When I am meeting people, learning what they are about, what they need and desire, when I see possible ways to help them.

"What's stopping you?"

By March 25, when I spoke with sensitive Kate Maxwell, another colleague from my coaching studies, Kate suggested that I release whatever "vow of poverty" I may have taken. If I were hanging on to such a paradigm, I was to let it go. Whatever I might want to offer, I should begin to offer it at its most basic, rather than wait.

By Easter morning, April 8, I was in conversation with Rev. Barbara Marie, the sensitive I mentioned earlier. It seemed such a gift to be able to receive guidance in the ways that she does, so I could not help but ask, "Wouldn't it be helpful if I heard voices?" In the middle of all my fear and distress, my instruction was to focus on my vision, trusting that a solution would appear and then watch for what was coming to me.

Within hours, I was hearing the audio message of Noah St. John, and I was asking for permission to get "unstuck." Noah St. John's experience resonated with my own experience. Noah found a solution to his experience of being stuck through his quantum-leap discovery of afformations. He shared that idea. I heard it, and it helped me break through a block I had using affirmations. After months of frustration, changes started to happen almost immediately.

CHAPTER 11

THE POWER OF POSITIVE QUESTIONS

Have you ever played the Why game as a child or with your own children? Eventually, after a never-ending series of questions, most adults weary of the questions. But what if learning to ask why questions with the right attitude were one of the most powerful skills you could ever master? Would you be more willing to play longer the next time?

What if we became aware that we have been ignorant of the power in the Bible verse "Ask, and you will receive; seek, and you will find; knock, and the door will be opened" (Matt. 7:7)? What if it really is as simple as "ask and it is given"? Would you pay more attention to what you were asking for?

What if the secret key to working with the subconscious mind is to ask, rather than to tell? What if how you ask makes a difference? What if we do not have to convince, but merely ask the subconscious to support our goals through the power of the right question with the right feeling? What if the question enables us to avoid mental conflict or argument?

Intrigued? So was I.

I use daily affirmations, but they often evoke a visceral reaction that does not feel right. The sensation is one of being caught in a lie. Others acknowledge similar experiences, yet affirmations and autosuggestions are the traditional teaching. At least, Sharon Wilson acknowledges this dishonest feeling and creates "progressive beliefs," revising a statement until we can comfortably affirm that which we desire.

So I found it very compelling when I was introduced to the work of Noah St. John. According to his story, he experienced the same physical sensations I felt when using affirmations. He had run into the same brick wall—until he fell upon a slightly different approach that changed everything for him and the people who work with him.

What St. John suggested was to use "afformations," a term coined to capture the essence of something in a state of forming or becoming, instead of an affirmation, a firm statement made regularly to convince the subconscious of its validity. The key to utilizing afformations was to ask oneself positive questions.

Everything that Bob Proctor had said to me became clear. The idea of using questions to access the subconscious was part of the success literature Bob had studied for the past fifty years. It went further. Any question sets the subconscious mind into motion, seeking answers and creating the circumstances to bring about a corresponding result—positive or negative.

What St. John was suggesting was that we should consciously flip any negative self-talk or "head trash" into positive why questions in order to activate the subconscious mind to our advantage. Within a few hours, I understood the basics of afformations.

The next step in Noah's program was to use them all the time. We were shown how to craft them and use recordings to keep up a continuous flow of positive why questions. I began to ask them, one after another. Why is life so good? Why do I have permission to succeed? Why is positive cash flow returning to my bank account? Why are my ideal clients suddenly around me? Why am I getting to spend time with my family? Why am I so blessed to live on this lovely ranch? Why am I so enthused and happy? Why do I have the artists and technicians around me to support my creations? Why are my presentations so much fun? Over the next few days, these questions were my focus. I began to feel confident that using afformations would yield results.

As I worked with afformations, I was struck by the number of questions I used every day, including a five-question power review designed to find solutions and reveal one action I could take the next day to improve my results and to feel the way I wanted to feel. I also thought about how often we complain about problems, turning them into negative questions. Ever hear yourself or others ask, "Why am I so stupid?" What if we did not need to condemn ourselves or blast others? What if it were simpler than that? What if results followed just by engaging the cooperation of the conscious and subconscious mind through the right questions? I remembered that Dr. Murphy taught that the answer is in every question—if you listen.

What if there were a better way to utilize the mind? What if the Biblical statement, "Ask and you shall receive" had, in fact, been a method to have the mind take over the work in the background with less effort on our part? What if asking the right questions were the key? Framed as afformations, this new concept felt like a powerful revelation. It felt like a quantum leap.

My conscious mind began to use questions to obtain choices and then explore positive options. I was ready to find a way to get unstuck. I opened to letting go of paradigms that certainly did not appear to be helping me achieve my goals—thoughts like: "I'm not qualified." "I don't have enough money." "I'm too old." "I don't know how." I started flipping my thinking.

Was I experiencing ambivalence or praying in two directions? Then I could write positive afformations to help me enjoy and care for my family. "Why is it so easy to enjoy my family?" "Why do I find ways to improve our environment daily?" "Why is it so easy to resolve contrasts?" Did I have doubts and other negative thinking as I pursued my goals? Afformations offered an alternative solution. "Why do I receive all the resources that I require?" "Why am I so richly blessed?"

"Why am I living my life purpose?" "Why am I doing my perfect work?" "Why am I such a success?" "Why am I so happy?" "Why is our lifestyle so improved?'

The question "What's stopping you?" flips into a positive question: "Why am I moving forward?"

"Why don't I have enough money" becomes "Why are my finances improving in such significant ways?"

For problems in the workplace: "Why does our work environment improve every day?" "Why are those around me so happy?" "Why do I see ways to help others live better?" "Why does this help me live better too?"

That first week, results were not visible in my outer world. My problems seemed as insurmountable as ever, but my mind was filled with questions. Within days, these questions began to propel me past stuck points. My journals were filled with them.

Why do questions work so well? Why does asking work? Why do afformations work so well? Why do I know what will move me forward toward my goals? Why do I feel so good?

There was a strong contrast between the immediate results I needed and the lack of any confirmation that they would appear. I was aware that benefits come from the willingness to choose actions in faith, so I crafted afformations to address that. Why do I trust God? Why do I believe that God is the source of my supply? Why do I reconcile my desire to write with the actions that bring me money? As I flipped my thinking to support my goals, I felt as if I had been invited to get out of my own way and play.

Words from one of the Abraham-Hicks daily e-mails stayed with me. They spoke about not creating through hard work or action alone. They said that we create through our sense of well-being and feeling good. The feeling vibration created calls forth actions that lead to more good feelings that come from what we want. So I wrote afformations about raising my vibration, on increasing financial supply and well-being, on clients and work. Why am I inspired to create as I write, coach, speak, and produce? Why is it so easy to do? Why have I found the brand that allows me to be truly me? Why does this help bring the center into being?

With my mind working on positive results, images began arriving in my meditations, guiding me to new ways to handle situations. While playing an Abraham-Hicks audio, I listened to a guided meditation about putting my boat into a great stream of desire. It resonated with me. I wrote my impression of it in my journal.

If you can imagine with me, "in the beginning, the stream is quiet. It's a gentle current moving me toward my destination. As I travel down the stream, my desire increases as I contemplate what I will find when I get there—and I find the current is getting stronger. The more I dream, the faster and more intense the current, generated by the emotions that exist in the gap between where I am and where I want to be. It is my passion fighting my frightened resistance that raises the waters to such an intense current.

"It grows to more than a stream; it's more like a river. In fact, it's the sensation of river rafting between the rocks. I'm in the rapids. I can't turn around and go back. I cannot fight the current. As it drives me forward, it's terribly uncomfortable. I try to resist, grabbing branches, logs, or anything that I might think will save me from the insistent drive forward. But the reality is that the current is too strong. It will push me forward. It is the hanging on while fighting the current that is painful. If I jump into the water, it will drain and terrify me, even tear me apart. "The best thing I can do is to stay in the boat (or get back into it), place a hand on the rudder to avoid the rocks around me, and enjoy the ride! There are opportunities and incredible insights to observe. I am in the rapids. I will get through them—and that's where the rewards are!"

A powerful lesson spoke to me: "Don't resist. Don't paddle against the current. Don't hang on to the branches. Let go and go with the flow. The faster you do this, the faster you can get through the rapids. Get into the boat. It's easier. My boat is in the river, oars up, riding the current. As I sit with only one finger on the rudder, keeping some bit of direction in the madness, I can observe the opportunities and resources around me."

I adjusted my daily morning meditation routine, incorporating both afformations and the boating image, and felt immediate relief. I was stunned by the rapid shift in a positive direction. Why was this? As I asked, the answer came. The subconscious *increases* or *enhances* what we think about. Fleeting thoughts have little impact, but dominant thoughts, especially those charged with emotion and belief, increase in the outer world without exercising any censorship. The idea that is realized is the one to which we give the most attention, toward our desires or away from them. If we don't like the results, then we need to review our thoughts and change them.

As I replayed the boating image, I found I could rewrite the mind movie, making adjustments to choose an easier way, to lighten my spirit and find new resources. These revised versions became new aha moments. I was becoming aware that I could choose an easier way. I could let go of what was holding me back. Whatever I thought about my ability to visualize before, I was actively engaged in playfully creating mental movies now.

Burt Goldman (creator, Quantum Jumping) tells us that when we use our imagination to play out a scene in our mind's eye, we see ourselves (or our "doppelganger") doing something. As our conscious mind merges with the moving picture, we create a memory picture to draw upon when we need it. As my own images played out, I found I was having fun!

Once I triggered this flow, I began to see and feel it all around me. It was a sensation of flying, a sense of serendipity, a chain of coincidences leading me in the desired direction. By now, I was on a roll. Memories from the past surfaced to remind me that I had lived through other experiences similar to what I had been feeling. When I was newly divorced, I had very little income. When Amy would come to visit, there were times when I had nothing to feed her but split-pea soup and egg noodles. She hated split-pea soup. There were those days in the Winnebago when we were out of food, fuel, and water—those weeks when we were down to our last $300. These were times when I had been unable to move forward and afraid to move back. In each of those instances, it had been difficult, but exhilarating, when I finally stepped into it and let go. The best things happened when I would get out of my own way.

Mentor Fawn Christianson had been the first to suggest when I was going through coaching training that I lighten up. I was in the "thought habit" of trying to maintain too much conscious control over any situation; it was a by-product of anticipating problems and solutions when managing television and feature film production. She wanted me to be aware that it's fine to consider multiple possibilities; however, if we allow our conscious mind to rule the day in all things, it's not unusual to find the intellect trying to impose reasoned solutions on the subconscious. Such mental effort can lead to the opposite of what we desire.

Hadn't I read Dr. Murphy's opinion that when prayers are not answered as we would like, the principal reason is often too much effort? It's easy to understand this. Have you ever been uncomfortable with someone hanging over your shoulder when you were trying to do something? Well, mentally straining endlessly to solve a problem, we're hovering next to our subconscious, giving it one suggestion after another and keeping it from getting on with its work.

I found a passage in Dr. Murphy's book *Think Yourself Rich* (p. 80):

Avoid struggle and strain. These are really signs of your unbelief. In your subconscious is all the wisdom and power necessary to solve any problem. Your conscious mind is prone to look at external conditions and tends continually to struggle and to resist. Remember, however, it is the quiet mind that gets things done.

I was receiving a clear message through my visualizations. Source, the stream of well-being and life force from which all that is flows, enjoys a light, joyful, and free creative experience. "The effortless way is best." "Relax. Easy does it." "Do not let yourself get bogged down in thinking about details and means." "Working harder does not lead to better results." "Willpower won't do it either."

Remember the image of my boat? Oars are up. No rowing is required. My sole involvement as I am carried along is to keep a finger on the rudder for a sense of direction. If the contrast I experience is too heavy, like an anchor weighing me down, then it is my job to identify the source of the burden and focus on eliminating that contrast first.

Whatever the laundry list of goals I had established, relieving this burden became my priority.

During these first days, the thought came to me repeatedly that the most important guideline for me was to ask: What lifts your spirit and moves you toward your goal? I also received another powerful piece of guidance: Watch for things in daily life that enable you to feel what you want to feel when you are living your dream. I was to find or recognize whatever simple ways came to me to accomplish this. What I would be doing was less important than how I was feeling. I was being asked to apply a light touch when thinking of my desires.

I wrote afformations about my primary goals; however, my journal revealed my doubts.

"I either stand on the leading edge of something incredible... or I'm crazy, being led down the cynic's path.... I am either laying the foundation to be well-equipped to coach the lookers and dreamers on how to understand their frustration, and pain in order to suggest that it is possible to come out the other side—or I have drunk the Kool-Aid.... If I can capture these feelings—the days of despair, the thoughts of quitting, alongside the pain of what failure would mean to me—then I can also show the other side—the role of afformations, affirmations, building belief, and keeping up persistent actions. I love you, Lord, and I believe."

I was grateful for my family, even though they gave no indication of providing loving support for my goals. "I want them to be proud of me, Lord," I wrote as I prepared to travel to yet one more marketing conference.

When I returned from the trip, my financial plight, like an anchor holding me back, represented the heaviest contrast I was experiencing, so this came first. I turned it over to my higher power. I meditated on possibilities and focused my afformations on the freedom and joy that solutions would produce.

I moved into activity mode for money—whatever it took. My inner thoughts focused on the book and center, while my outer activity was focused on resolving my financial crisis, completing numerous applications, and posting services online.

By establishing milestones by which to recognize successful movement, I would be able to see what the immediate end result would be and how I would feel as I reached it. So, following the writings of Jack Canfield mentioned earlier, I created a wheel to monitor paying down financial obligations. At its center was my goal: "Paid in Full." A larger wheel surrounded it, divided into sections, each representing one of my obligations. Each time a balance was paid, I would celebrate with a gold star. Like a small child, I looked forward to the moment when I could check off each small success with my reward. The wheel would be a scorecard, similar to a milestone map, which would also help keep me enthusiastically focused on my larger goal.

I continued to write afformations about my business expanding, communicating the principles of deliberate creation, and resources always coming to me at the right time and place. I continued to journal: Ask and it is given—"and I am asking now, Lord, for the resources to continue the work I have been blessed to pursue, to travel, and to publish the book when it's ready. Why do I know the perfect way to share this message?"

My purpose might be to communicate the creative process; however, my work involved maintaining the self-discipline to take persistent actions toward that goal so that those who wanted to become aware of it would connect with me. Large visions require many small goals to attain them.

Each day I was consciously integrating what I had been learning of the creative process. Ask the subconscious to link to an expansive, creative, quantum force; then relax, let go, and await a response with positive expectation, one of the most powerful emotions we can use to trigger positive results. It is a technique the Bible and the ancients understood. As you ask, be open to receive and be prepared to get into motion when the answer comes. It may come from an entirely different direction than you expected, so it's important to be open to follow the direction you receive, even from the most unlikely source.

It was a confusing time. I was randomly looking for sales or production jobs, and struggling to grapple with so many conscious questions about all the things I had been doing... Sometimes you just have to ask your conscious mind to be quiet.

So nearly one month after hearing about afformations, that's what I did. I went into the silence. No more input from television or the computer—just centered silence. I listened to the questions that emerged.

"What is your greatest gift? If you had plenty of money, what would you do?" I'd spend my time writing, finding content to publish, and then produce. I'd hire a staff and assistant to edit, lay out, produce, and market. I'd speak and guide.

"What's stopping you now?" The hole I dug financially.

"Can you find a producing or publishing gig that matches this vision?" Quite possibly.

"What do you need?" A paying gig. Lord, I will accept what comes my way—production or sales.

For several weeks, my outer life revolved around insurance and sales, but I was drawn to creating content. I enjoyed the writing and publishing process. I had enjoyed the past year because I had been writing or helping to write. When had I felt the best? When I was running, organizing, presenting, and doing the required work to make it happen.

"Susan, ask people—they may not be aware of your work. You write, speak, and produce, but you have to find a mechanism to get it out there! You don't know if there is a reward at the end of the rainbow, but do it anyway."

I was grateful for the inner stillness to hear my heart. To change, one has to be willing to do whatever it takes, and that requires being open to finding the money to pay for all that is required, no matter where it might originate.

By the one month "afformation" anniversary, no miracles or magical manifestations had appeared; however, the questions had helped. I was feeling better. I acknowledged my joy in guiding others to discover that they too can create through their physical reality. I wanted to write and share that everybody has the potential to align to source and accomplish their dreams if they have the two key components: stay focused on the energized vision while enjoying the journey, and maintain persistent, consistent activity—at least one thing daily that makes them feel as they want to feel.

I set out my five-year vision in all areas of my life again. Finances were first: a regular income-earning activity to be on sound footing financially. My family and lifestyle were important: the time to visit with Amy, Tom, and Charlie, the ranch in order, and the ability to travel. It was not about titles or target dates, although they were a way of demonstrating progress. Rather it was about pursuing my purpose: communicating and providing access to the creative process, whether guiding, creating personal development content, or being part of a conference center. When I had completed the plan, from the grand vision to the moment-by-moment choices required to get me there, I released it all. I turned it over to my subconscious mind to see what would unfold according to the law of gestation. Some things take time to develop.

It was time to do some mental housekeeping. I knew that paradigms could impede our progress if they no longer serve us. One of mine was the belief that I had to be successful to prove the creative process. Instead, I flipped my thinking to what success felt like to me. It was a sense of accomplishment. As I focused on this one feeling, things started to surge ahead without pushing on my part. I saw the next steps—finish the writing, send it out to a few trusted colleagues, and when it feels right, physically publish it.

Physical housekeeping accompanied the mental. I thought about the stockpile of papers I still stored from previous shows. Not only were they a great pile of clutter dragging me down physically; they were also old projects I wanted to leave behind. So into the closets and cabinets I went to toss the old to make room for the new! It wouldn't all be gone in a day, but it was a start.

My journal noted: "It's time for cord cutting!!! Study and let go of that which holds me to the past. So today, I pry my fingers off the trapeze bar and let myself fall into Thy loving net. I step off the platform and enjoy the swing—the rush of air, the exhilaration."

It was a good time to clear away that which no longer served, and so, with gratitude, I began clearing away old e-mails as well. I had already decided clearing would be a big part of the next thirty days… eliminating the good in order to make room for the great. There is something liberating about letting go, even though I still have to remind myself not to grab it back. I wanted to feel clear, receptive, enjoying the ride, comfortable where I am, releasing the past so I can embrace the new energies coming to me.

On a daily basis, ideas and questions surfaced on the journal pages: "The creative process is really elegantly simple. See what you want. Plan what needs to happen to receive it. Do those things. Review the results. Could it be any simpler? Then what stops so many people? They get distracted."

At that point, my emotional distress over my finances was certainly a distraction, but I kept up my prayers and afformations. Gradually, my focus shifted. "There is a time to learn and a time to let go of the instruction manual and just do it, be it." I could be supported doing what I love, allowing it to unfold according to Divine plan. "I trust Thee. I love Thee, Lord."

I began to realize that my ideal clients were everywhere, each connected to the creative nature of quantum consciousness, each doing his or her part to create and expand. My task was to encourage them. The book was the immediate goal. I would be shown the next step on the journey when others had it in hand:

"It isn't about me. It is about a space where people can learn to translate visions into a plan… to work through the contrasts.… What if the center is an incubator, a living example of a business campus that supports the holistic well-being of its community? What would that look like?"

A small amount of money came in from location scouting and serving as a poll worker, enough for me to feel comfortable paying a few bills. Although I was grateful, I was also impatient, so I had to remember to keep my life and will in God's care. Whatever was happening, it seemed to be out of my control… "Please show me how I may serve, for it is all beyond me… What is the lesson here? Lighten up, let go. Go with the flow and hold the vision to allow all to work out." As a mental time-out, I began to play the prosperity game, in which you see yourself receiving imaginary sums and spending it that day. The next day the amount doubles, and you imagine how to spend that sum as well. The amounts keep doubling each day as long as you play the game. I would spend the first $1,000 on a trip to Seattle to see the kids; $2,000 to get the house spiffed up; $4,000 to pay bills; $8,000 on an event. I could even see how it would occur:

As we gathered, we would meditate, then split up into small groups, each with a facilitator, where all could express ideas about what they hoped to accomplish. I would invite people to dream. I would talk about how dreams progress, how the work of the center is to follow up and help them hold the dream. I would come away energized. Participants would come away with a progressive "business" plan—the product, the team, the marketing, the operations, as well as tools designed to help them work through the beliefs, fears, and obstacles that get in the way. We'd encourage them to work with people to help them through the contrasts and challenges, knowing that as we define the contrast, we may reshape the vision and the path to its accomplishment without losing the dream. We'd tell them: "Focus on the dream. Align with it. The universe will attract the 'what and how.' That is none of your business."

I kept playing. $16,000 was next, enough to spend four months working on the book or take some special vacation with my family; $32K to get rid of what drags me down; $64K, to do the feasibility study for the center.

There were long-term financial goals: pay down the burden of obligations, purchase an annuity, then assets that contribute income, educational funds for Charlie, and money to build the center. Peter wanted to pay down the mortgage and buy a ranch adjacent to the big ranch. Anything was possible in the game. Who knew? It might be possible to buy a big ranch with hundreds of acres and turn it into the center.

For a time, I was at the wildest expansion of possibilities: options for financial resources, shows, and other content to develop that could contribute to a lifestyle I was designing around the ranch and my family, but where did it all fit together? To have so much going on was a distraction, yet I held the center, an image of the book, and afformations in mind.

Author Claude Bristol (*The Magic of Believing*) asks us to focus on that which we desire more than anything else and write a brief word picture. I noted in my journal: "Mine is centered on the center. It is so real on the inner planes—and all that I am becoming, all that I seek to do, is perceived as steps along the journey. Sometimes the details become too dense and I get lost in the 'how,' but I have a powerful servomechanism that centers me, aligns me, and helps me focus."

One of the neat things about all the clearing I had been doing was that it took little thoughtful concentration. That freed me to apply laser focus and attention on the relationship between the person who could found the center and the author, producer, and guide I was becoming. Were there contrasts? Absolutely. I was grateful for a sense that each goal achieved could move me closer to the center, with the potential to touch millions of lives, one at a time. I was at once holding the grand vision and allowing resources to play out through the next-presented, bite-size chunks. They didn't all make sense in the moment, but I had faith that eventually they would. Occasionally, I would get a glimpse into how the dots might all come together. I was aware that the center was more than a retreat and conference center; it was also a dream incubator, a "hatchery." These glimpses would reenergize my creative efforts to get busy.

Almost two months had passed since I heard of afformations. They were having an effect on how I approached each day. My inner focus was on the work of the center—incubating dreams, founding it, making money. What did I need to do? What did I need to clear to allow the next step of the journey? I was grateful for what I perceived to be my part in the ongoing expansion and creation of something new… the book… a program… a space like Omega in Massachusetts, Whidbey Island in Washington, or Asilomar in California to incubate dreams… a distribution arm like Hay House.

My outer activity was on learning scripts and setting appointments for sales work. It was clear that at some point, this had to move to the next level. "That point is now," I wrote. As usual, I was asking questions—but not about sales and not always as afformations. I needed to remember to ask in the right way.

At the two-month afformations mark, my primary concern was still to earn money. All other goals and concerns fell back. Small bits of minimum-wage work began to arrive. It was not much, but it provided gas for the car and the chance to choose my own menu. My days were simple—telemarketing, listening to sales scripts, accompanying the sales managers on calls, and clearing the house. It gave me the essentials and a bit of a reality check. Insurance would consist of the same challenges I was experiencing in network marketing. I decided to put all sales activities on hold and focus on more substantial, faster cash returns.

Still writing, I asked: How can I help others to shift from "going through the motions, doing all the right things" to "become" that which they seek? What is the trigger, the source of the shift? This is where we persist in our outer activity while we either catch up internally or relinquish control to allow ourselves to be guided to something better than we imagined.

During a lull from all the activity, I had a chance to lunch with the wife of one of Peter's Buckaroos. Karen H. was going through her own research about where to take her career. We had a great visit, and I came away with one very down-to-earth suggestion. If the large center were too out of reach to be believable, could I not picture a small, existing building with interior courtyard gardens, where a co-op of service providers could have offices, much like my Film Offices Plus incubator from years before? As everyone shared space, they could lead workshops, seminars, music therapy, movement, and art—just like the grand vision but on a smaller scale. I played with it, thinking about a way station where people could come to rest, play, rejuvenate, and hear the stories of others who had gone ahead. It would help them get prepared for their own journey.

I had reached a point where my life was about being, becoming, persisting in the doing, and applying. Ultimately the process exists whether we acknowledge it or not. All I could do was to share, provide access, and help people pop paradigms. I was so tired of listening to myself on the theory, the constant dissecting of the process and how it relates to me. I wrote: "It's time to live in the choices I make. It's time to let go and enjoy the ride! I am where I am. I gave myself permission to do this. I am positioned now, as uncomfortable as it may be, to make the choices that lead me toward my vision or away. If it's right, we feel good. If in a different direction, we are aware of contrasts."

I was experiencing a strong contrast between the creative I wished to capture and the sales I felt I should do. Another friend, Beth, called, and as the three months' afformation anniversary approached, I was choosing between opportunities. It was a hard decision. I had been working so hard in the direction I thought held the most future promise, even though it had not yet yielded any financial results. The other choice would take me back into production, on a show I knew nothing about. Would it be more of what I had been seeking to escape? I was torn. Would the financial benefit that dovetailed with my primary goal at the moment outweigh the time I had put into building something new? I knew that I had to let go on this. I had said I would do whatever it took to work through the financial issues, receive funds to resolve my obligations, and build a residual base.

The new "how" was coming from a different direction than I had been seeking. Was I able to make just one requirement? I wanted to be able to coach creative people to make "it" happen, to get from where they are to where they want to be. I also wanted good money.

"The center begins within."

Will it become the beautiful building I've envisioned?

"That remains to be seen." For now, finding a space to co-op is a beginning, a place to invite others to see their dream and become part of it, to give talks and to see what it takes to help support them.

I began to realize how important afformations were to me. Rather than anticipating problems, I wanted to define opportunities. So I wrote new afformations: Why do I only see the opportunities and resources in people, places, and things? Why do I see ways to improve areas of contrast easily and effortlessly? Why do I celebrate the finest financial solution for the near- and short-term, feeling joy, clarity, enthusiasm, and relief?

My financial journey had humbled me, and as I faced this new choice, I turned to Peter for his opinion. I did not want to risk his well-being in pursuit of my own. Peter does not believe in "iffy" things.

He could not have made his opinion known more clearly. "Take the money."

The message of the boating visualization came again: Stop trying to swim upstream against the current. Everything we want is downstream. Again, as the movie replayed as part of my journaling. I was in the water again, hanging onto the branches. Each time I would let go, the violence of the current would frighten me, and I would grab the branches instinctively to save myself. I became aware that I had been hanging onto the way I had consciously decided was the path forward, instead of embracing a new, unexpected opportunity. It was holding me back. And the harder I held on, in spite of my desire to move downstream, the more rapid and violent the current in which I found myself.

I realized that I could get into the boat where it was more comfortable. A rope was still holding the boat to shore, and the anchor was still dragging it down. So I cast off and pulled up the anchor. Whoosh! What a fabulous, freeing sensation! I was moving. I wasn't stuck in the rocks along the shore any longer! But rowing was hard work; the current was strong. All I had to do was lift up my oars and enjoy the ride. What a fantastic shift! I was flowing downstream, enjoying the view. The current was still strong, taking me toward my next destination; however, it was safe and enjoyable. What freedom! I was feeling happy, joyous, and free!

By hanging onto an image we have, it is possible to close off an incredible opportunity, an alternative choice of which we are unaware. This is not to be interpreted as "giving up" one's dreams. Rather, it is a suggestion that we allow for something better and invite the subconscious to offer options if any are available. I have to admit that sometimes the suggestions delight me. Other times, I am tempted to say, "You've got to be kidding."

In this case, when the universe moved to bring me options that had the power to resolve contrasts, it was not a time to look a gift horse in the mouth, especially when I had been in a slump and asking for help. It was a time to stay open to receive what was coming my way. I took the show.

CHAPTER 12

PLAYING IN GOD'S GARDENS

As soon as I began the new show, I felt tremendous gratitude and relief. The immediate work was in hand—to create our production space and line up our crew. It felt vacuous after pushing hard for so long. Perhaps that was the point. An empty space had opened, and Nature would rush in to fill it, depending upon the images I held. For now, I relished the relief from financial pressures. It freed my spirit. My thoughts were on satellite trucks and wireless transmissions.

Although I continued to journal and write afformations in support of my long-term goals, I had far less time to do it. The majority of the week was consumed pulling together what had to be built before we started to tape. We had to hire a creative staff and crew and provide them with places to work. We had to bring in the basic bio-services such as restrooms, snack services, catered meals and a space to serve those, supplies, office equipment, phones, and Internet. Our first location lacked basic utilities. We were building an infrastructure from scratch.

Our production army required buildings, or in this case, trailers. We had to bring in an entire complex to house executive and producer offices, hair and makeup, wardrobe, art department, dressing rooms and "star trailers," engineering, control room, and edit bays. The house that became our studio needed to be outfitted with lights, audio and camera cabling, and set dressing. We would need two kitchens to serve the television cooking segments. The backyard with its small outdoor stage needed to be relandscaped. And as the piece de resistance, we needed to connect to fiber cables on the studio lot in order to make daily digital delivery to the network for broadcast each morning. Walking down our "street" at dusk one evening when it was finally in place, I felt a powerful sense of accomplishment.

People in the film industry make these things happen regularly; however, it was still a large undertaking, and it was all I could do to find time to afform the book in my morning journals. Writing had to take a backseat—something to do on weekends. For months, the center slipped out of sight.

Our focus shifted to establish systems and routines for the project. This was a daily show. It needed to establish a rhythm—its natural habitforce—in order to relieve the stress of creating two hours of programming Monday through Friday, week in and week out, over the coming year. Under our executives' leadership, regular daily meetings, rehearsals, and taping provided a structure for the creative staff. Even the production team had such rhythms, from the production assistants who came in early to set up coffee and "craft service" to the detailed accounting processes that made the financial cycles flow so well. I was extremely fortunate to have a solid team by my side.

I was still experiencing contrasts in my personal life. My financial woes did not magically disappear, but afformations provided a tool with which to face them. Whenever I experienced the physical discomfort of a contrast, I could flip the thought and turn it into a positive question: Why did my checkbook have more funds in it? Why was I able to bring each account current? After that, I would imagine the thrill of accomplishment in restoring my financial well-being and leave the job of bringing about my visualizations to my subconscious mind.

From my perspective as I lived the experience, the steps of the creative process sounded simple, in and of themselves. All of us have an inherent ability to create. The primary challenge is to focus on one thing long enough to bring it into being without trying to control the results.

Put it in the context of quantum physicist Goswami's description of the creative process (see my model below):

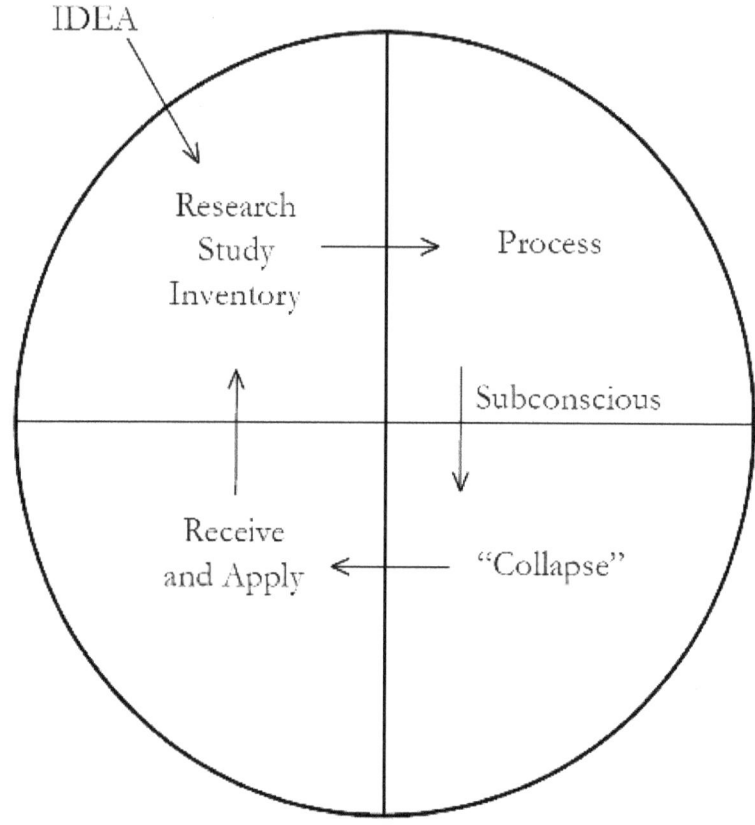

Quantum Creative Process

Everything begins as a thought associated with a desire, a question, or a contrast. Concentrating on this idea, we activate the possibility of actually creating what we think and feel in our own experience. We research possible solutions to the problem as the conscious mind continues to work toward a solution. We focus on it. If no immediate answer is forthcoming, individuals turn it over to the subconscious mind for "unconscious processing."

Some people "sit for ideas" in a meditative state like Thomas Alva Edison. Others stop working and take a walk, go to the beach, watch a movie, or ride a bicycle. The goal is to let go of conscious effort. The amount of time required varies greatly, but suddenly, an insight "collapses" into the conscious mind. It may seem to come out of nowhere or as a result of an object in their environment triggering a connection to the problem at hand. Their aha insight helps them move back into action, solution in hand. No coercion or demanding is required. In fact, it helps to be playful.

So, if the process is so simple, why isn't everybody doing it? To use a sporting analogy, they take their eye off the ball. They get distracted. They pay more attention to how to swing the club rather than looking at where they want the ball to go.

Imagine that your attention is focused on the obstacles blocking the way to what you want. Not only are you no longer concentrating on the goal; you are focusing on the exact opposite. The subconscious mind simply accepts and reacts to what it is given. It does not pick and choose among different courses of action. It is like a garden in which you plant seeds all day long in complete faith that according to the laws of nature if you plant an apple seed, you will grow an apple tree. So it is with thoughts and statements.

When you plant positive seed thoughts, you receive positive results—like to like. That's why Dr. Joseph Murphy (author, *The Power of Your Subconscious Mind*) made the point that "your job is with the conscious mind." Not only do we want to make sure the right thoughts are given to the subconscious mind; we also want to train the conscious mind to stay focused on its desired results. As long as we have desires and contrasts, we will continue to grow freely toward them.

What idea first engaged me? It was an evolving sense of purpose to share something that millions of people do not know about the power of their minds to create. Throughout my story, the vision morphed from its early expression as a retreat center. It was part of the criteria we considered when buying our new ranch. I saw it as a place for inner and outer exploration, filled with music, movement, the arts, and themed gardens to open each guest to the fields of possibility.

At this first stage of creation, I had resonated with an idea and then begun to research and take inventory of what I already had to support the dream. I knew about creating content for radio and television. I had become a coach trained in the creative success process. I saw how a combination of guiding, writing, and producing could lead to the center.

My description of my vision combined with my feelings to become an archetypal blueprint. According to Amit Goswami, quantum consciousness uses such "energetic blueprints" to create everything. The vision will be incomplete at the start, but preparatory research and inner work help develop the idea and provide possible avenues to its successful creation.

The show was scheduled to shoot for almost a full year. With production filling most of my waking hours, I knew my vision would have to be a work in progress, and that would require focus, using the tools I had learned to hold a steady course.

I disciplined myself to get up an hour early to meditate so I could hold my long-term visions as laid out on my milestone map. At the far end of the map, the center seemed distant and out of focus, but the book was still a part of the end results that I could keep doing. What had started as an outline had grown and expanded. It was more tangible. I could believe in the possibility of publishing it by working on weekends. Coming from an operations background, I could see milestones to check off as they were accomplished: the writing, the next steps to publish, and launch. On the map, these actions led to more books, a program to design, video content to create, entertaining talks to deliver, events to attend as participant or invited guest, and residual income to develop.

During that time, conscious thought was interacting with the subconscious. I asked my subconscious questions, using afformations, imagining what it would feel like when I accomplished my dreams, listening for guidance as to what would help me feel that way each day. My imagination in full gear, I might see a mind movie, layering details into my vision, surrounding it with feeling, allowing thoughts to drift by without the need to grasp or scheme.

All my physical spaces provided me with visual cues, ranging from index cards and vision boards to the chaotic pile of research materials that filled my work space at home. I was confident that it was sufficient to hold the vision of my book while waiting for comments. My subconscious would work it out. I was grateful for any indication that the book was moving closer to reality. I had been granted the awareness to get out of my own way. I had been blessed with creative inspiration and intuition in every aspect of my life—from the book to the show—and it was all progressing in an orderly fashion.

I scheduled a minimum of one morning each weekend to the work and kept writing. I also saved most of the techniques designed to keep an idea in front of us and underscore our faith that we "will until" for weekends. They included maintaining associations, working with mentors, studying, doing exercises, and creating charts, plans, and pictures.

I eliminated less important projects to improve my focus as time became a more precious commodity. The work was about how to convey the playful, joyful quality of creativity to bring joy to others. I looked for games and tools to play with the subconscious. In the spirit of play, I asked people to tell me their favorite games, and I would put colorful images of them on my bulletin board. It's not about the games; it's about the way we feel when we see and play them.

My wish list was still out there, yet by fall, in the span of six months after beginning to work with afformations, my finances had improved dramatically. It was possible to think of visiting and feel the joy of being with Amy, Tom, and Charlie regularly.

My journals continued to reflect next steps: "My job is to hold the vision that this or something better is coming." What brought me the most joy? Writing. As we prepared to enter actual production, I received a job promotion, and the resulting pay increase would cover the anticipated cost of publishing the book. "I am where I am, and it's okay."

Just before cameras were set to roll, imagine my joy as I completed the book's first draft. I still wanted to do a second draft and share it with a few people close to me before I went in search of a publisher. Still, we were so busy creating the new show that there was just enough time to pray, journal, glance at my milestone map, and focus on the immediate task at hand daily.

Napoleon Hill felt this internal action separates those who drift through life from those who live with purpose. I see it as the very essence of persistence. We want to create the habit of thinking about our vision, focusing on the long-term results we want, daily. Holding the thought is a persistent action that sets up a vibration of attraction. People may not see it or know what it is, but they will feel and be drawn to its energy. It isn't just about imagining a picture; it's about feeling its reality regardless of the outer circumstances around us. It is then that the power of our subconscious responds to our conscious choice. I believe that is how we pray without ceasing. It connects us to quantum consciousness. I was delighted that the show turned out to be positive and informative. Expressions of gratitude and afformations came in handy in the workplace, for if I began to over think a situation or technical aspect of the show, I could flip my thinking, focus on the success of the show, and turn it over to the subconscious mind. When the details of building threatened to overwhelm me, I did just that, trusting that solutions were there and all would work out. I could see phase one of my plans coming together.

Weeks became months. There were several things to do to feel good and be motivated in my existing environment as I continued to focus on and enjoy the creativity of the day-to-day producing process and worked with our staff, guests, and a wide variety of people involved in the broadcast and promotion of the show. I was looking forward to enjoying my home, lifestyle, and family. Surrounded by creativity in an atmosphere of fun, I found I did not have to wait for the center to be built or the book published to enjoy living my purpose.

As the weeks passed, I received intangible results as well—insights into the process, the subconscious, and the tools:

I was learning to play with my subconscious. How easy it is to create when we play as children. We are not attached to the results for any length of time. We go to the beach and build a sand castle. We squeal and scream as the waves come in and undo our work. Rarely do we sit down defeated. Rather, we gather our tools and build it again. Laughing, we watch for the next waves, scatter as they burst again upon our design, and continue the game of creating and recreating. It may be more challenging as adults, but when we work together, utilizing the power of the mastermind and caring for one another, we manage. New opportunities even allow us to build bigger and better as we release the way it was for the way it may be.

I found ways to prime the creative imagination when words did not flow. I too can be overwhelmed with too many details to do much dreaming. I used guided meditations, such as a collection in *Meditations for Daily Joy* by my friend Genevieve Gerard. One particular meditation, called "Scrambled Eggs," was a rampage of gratitude to be done while in activities such as making coffee or washing the dishes. It gets us in touch with our creative imagination as we express gratitude for all that is necessary to bring us the eggs, coffee, or clean sink. Feelings of gratitude help us align with quantum consciousness.

As I played with my imagination, feeling my way, I found I was building a relationship with my higher self, my subconscious, in an effortless way. Playing together, ideas began to flow freely toward desires held. Playing with my subconscious, I felt linked to the creative nature of the life force.

When we play, we alter our physical and thought patterns, leaving behind the stresses and pressures of daily life, to suspend what we call reality. Instead, we focus on the activity of the game. As we let go of our conscious control over the outcome, the nonconscious mind accesses alternative ideas from the field of possibility and begins to funnel them to us.

I learned to allow myself to receive the ideas. Sometimes, when I wanted to make a direct, conscious connection, I would use centered prayer or take an inspirational book such as *Port Hueneme Beach Walks: My Path to Peace,* written by my colleague Sondra Briggs, on a walking meditation.

I began to feel that we can get much further, faster, if we release the compulsive need to know and control the outcome of our ideas. It's fun to toss these ideas around, exploring what we feel about them, expressing approval when we receive one we like, passing others by that we don't like. It expands our thinking beyond the limits of our conscious mind. There is another benefit as well. When we resonate with ideas coming from the subconscious, we feel the expansive creativity in our immediate surroundings. When our feelings are engaged, we discover what we can do in our current environment to move toward our vision.

The creative process involves conscious thinking, outer activities, and inner feelings. I found it most helpful to begin by focusing on my feelings, allowing them to help me define my game plan. The feelings are the energy of the blueprint, which helps us identify the actions that provide a direct path to our desires. Some actions will lead to these desires. Others will not. Our task is to identify which is which so that we can take appropriate actions. If we have taken the time to allow our vision to expand, we know what we want and why, what it looks like and feels like, and what we will do with it when we have it. We even know what it feels like when we do not have it. This process can take some time—or happen in the blink of an eye. We do not know how or when. In fact, the subconscious mind has no sense of time, so there is no need to hurry the building of a vision. Time and pressure are of our own making.

Using a milestone map, dream board, or mind movie involves laying out the steps and filling them in with pictures, symbols, special words, family pictures, and meaningful book covers. If a large series of steps has to occur, such as a course of study, research may be required. Sometimes I'll lay out a path from the end backward: "Before I could do this, I would need to do…" I journal while creating the steps in order to describe the desired feeling experience from each step's accomplishment, as well as identifying what could be done today that would help me feel that way immediately. My map is a path, but you might like a chart representing different areas of your life that all need to move forward together to achieve your goals. For the sake of simplicity, I roll all my ideas into a symbol to hold that helps me review, affirm, and visualize my goals every day.

We want things because we resonate with an essence we perceive in them. It is entirely possible that this may come to us from a completely different source, a kind of serendipity that surprises us or bypasses the path we expected. Things happen, including unexpected surprises. They may help us skip several steps or send us back several steps. They may exact a toll or earn us extra resources. The point is to enjoy the creative process. Get up, show up, do the work, and allow the results to play out.

You may have noticed by now that I like to incorporate a vision of a journey that resonates with me, like building a bridge to cross the gap or getting ready to steer my boat downstream. Others come to mind: climbing a mountain or sitting in a boardroom. I find that as I go through lists and images, sorting them by category and prioritizing them, I get a sense of the lifestyle they are describing that is like a photo being developed, emerging onto the paper. I may move the images around and find that some elements demand my attention immediately, while some of the dreams feel like rewards for accomplishing something more pressing or more important on the list.

I note my feelings repeatedly. Occasionally, an idea pulls me off into a mind movie, and I let it flow, enjoying positive feelings, letting negative emotions pass quickly.

Asking positive questions on a daily basis, I learned that my subconscious mind collaborates in pictures. It brought to mind Genevieve Behrend's experience with mental visualization in the early 1900s. The only pupil of New Thought educator Thomas Troward, she described her process to become his student in her book *Your Invisible Power*. One of the key elements was to use the mind to vividly picture what she wanted. Night after night, she would picture herself walking the deck of the steamer that would be required to carry her from the United States to the United Kingdom, where Troward resided. She would picture herself receiving the monies required to make the journey. She also quoted a Thomas Troward affirmation. I found it so meaningful that I repeat a paraphrased version daily: My mind is a center of Divine operation ever seeking growth, expansion, and the creation of something entirely new, proceeding in an orderly fashion out of that which has gone before.

In Acts 17:28, God/source/life force was referred to as "That in which we live and move and have our being." This description, in conjunction with Troward's words, became a powerful affirmation of my relationship with source, of the never-ending will of life force to expand and create through each and every living being. It reinforced the power of intuition to inspire and guide me to create as well. Inspired, it is as if I become the instrument of this universal creative mind, free to choose or not to choose any given idea.

For those who live with their feet planted firmly on the ground, believing only what their senses tell them, communication with the subconscious mind may be overlooked because it answers us in ways we may not realize. When I began to watch for this, I could be more receptive when it happened. I often feel led to a bookstore, where I may pick up a book or overhear a conversation that provides insights that solve a problem. I could dismiss them as coincidental; however, this is frequently how the subconscious reaches into the world of our active senses. I may hear something on the radio, find a phrase in a book or online, or contemplate the symbolism in a deck of cards or an artistic creation that moves me toward a solution. It might also happen through song lyrics, conversations, or chance encounters. One question may lead to an answer, which then yields image after image, leading me to capture them in a mind map or brainstorm, jumbled pages of circled words that land on the space without reason.

Dialogues with the subconscious may begin while using a guided meditation that takes off in its own direction, like the boating example I previously shared. As we reinforce the inner movie with outer pictures in the environment, including ourselves in the experience, we trigger the mind movie's power. Physical representations of the inner thoughts contribute to our inner image of desired result. We may not take it in consciously every time we see it, but it works in the background, reinforcing our idea each time our eye passes by it. As I go through this process, immersing myself in images, a dialogue begins with the subconscious.

At first, I may be led to follow a mentor, work with a sales manager, or apprentice to a master or a millionaire, who can provide the experiences that fill in the gap between learned knowledge and useful action. As we tag along with role models, observing how they spend their days and where they spend their money, the subconscious can weave a reality from these clues and reveal activities for us to follow. I begin to watch for ideas that can be translated into actions. The fastest way to a good, solid collaboration with our subconscious is to follow those suggestions. Do the next-presented thing and let the universe sort it out.

Do I always get the message? No. All those obstacles like resistance, hanging on too tight, and the thoughts I throw in my own way may interfere with the communication. I may still persist in the negative habit force of thoughts and beliefs that prevent me from seeing or hearing what is all around me. I may be afraid to take the training wheels off the bike and just allow an experience to yield up its treasures. That's why we need new ways to clear the way. Those new ways may not appear to have anything to do with what we desire. They may be more about breaking up our existing thought patterns. Our landslide, hitting bottom, or a more positive experience like paragliding may be our breakthrough experience.

I was fortunate to know Betty A., who left her first husband at age fifty-five. After she almost died because he would not take her to the hospital during an appendicitis attack, she had an epiphany and began to prepare herself for the split. When finally divorced, she found herself watching paragliding on the beach of Cancun (in and of itself a breakthrough experience). For whatever crazy, inspired reason, she decided to try it. It was awesome. She overcame her fear and flew. She told me that she heard Peter Pan singing "I'm flying" and was overcome with this incredible sense of freedom, flight, and release as all the stuff related to the divorce slipped away. Making that change in her life was the best thing she had ever done and opened her up to achieve a career and find a new significant other. At seventy-five, her life was a reflection of living her passion and following her heart!

Was she working hard at her plan in that moment? No, she was releasing the outcome, letting go, allowing herself to experience the richness of that moment. When we open to the possibility that an adventure could yield new treasures regardless of fear or discomfort, we are allowing ourselves to receive that which is given. It is all around us.

And we never know what it might yield. If we release the outcome and become available to possibility, the entire universe can present itself at our feet.

As I made my way through this journey, I came to understand that it was not about the lists I was making, the accomplishments or ranks I wanted to achieve, the goals I was placing on the calendar, the pictures of things on my vision board, or the wish list I was requesting. It was about the feelings, qualities, and essence that all of those things represented. It was about asking to feel that way, because the subconscious responds to why we want those things and the feelings we want to experience. Here's an exercise I found useful:

Start to journal about a specific contrast, then imagine what you would prefer and feel its reality, the thrill of accomplishment or the congratulations you will receive. Imagine receiving hugs and handshakes from close friends and family, seeing joy or pride registered in their faces. Become aware of how you have helped improve a situation. Make the picture vivid. Hear the voices; see the gestures. Why do you want that? What does it mean in your life? How does it make you feel? What could you do to experience those feelings right now? Why is it possible? Ask the questions, and the subconscious brings about the realization of the strongest emotionalized desire. All that is needed comes about. It is the experience and joy of "answered prayer."

But what about those things beyond our life experience? For now, they are symbols of what you believe. What is it you imagine they will bring to you? What in your environment includes those feelings? Have you ever felt that way before? When? Remember how that felt and associate it with your vision. If you have felt that way before, you can feel it again. Is it okay to be where you are right now, feeling this feeling? Can you take pleasure from this now while everything else is coming to pass?

Accepting where we are even as we envision an improved future is like living in dramatic beats, the way an actor lives a script, segment by segment, moment by moment, never chewing off more than he or she can handle. As each event occurs, we ask, "What is it I want now? How do I want to feel as I eat lunch, meet a friend, have a conversation, work, or create around me? Is it possible to script the scene out in my head before it actually happens?"

What if I could pretend to have the people and resources around me to accomplish all the things I need or want to accomplish? I would never be overwhelmed. I could have the staff to handle the things I didn't enjoy. I could delegate the things I didn't have time to do to a manager who would handle the routine situations and only bring things that required my attention to me. I could pick and choose the things I wanted to do in a day and turn the rest over to the universe or my "power team" to do. And once I turned everything over, I could focus on how I would feel and get out of the way to allow it all to happen.

By year's end, I had received supportive responses to the first draft of the book, had gone through the second draft, and had chosen a publisher. Allowing a bit more time to massage the words, I finally submitted the manuscript for editorial comments. I had written a few paragraphs for one of Noah St. John's new books. I was thrilled when he asked if he could interview me. This was the life of published authors, and I was part of it.

As I waited for editorial notes, I promised myself that I would be open to them. I even went so far as to visualize each note as someone in my virtual audience asking a question for me to answer. This turned out to be a good attitude with which to face the notes that came back to me. There were hundreds of questions, and on my schedule, my publishing target date might have to be pushed back.

CHAPTER 13

LIVING THE CREATIVE LIFESTYLE

Where were you when you began to read my story? Perhaps you were curious about the title. Perhaps a friend recommended you read it. Perhaps something resonated with you as you glanced at the back cover. If you have come this far in the telling, some aspect of starting over after the landslide rang true to you. You may be facing a similar life crisis, with old patterns destroyed and no sense of the next steps required to rebuild your life. Perhaps your feelings were exposed and raw as you coped with a variety of problems on multiple fronts—financial, emotional, and physical. We did not know where to turn for the solutions that would help rebuild our world. You may feel that way too. Your heart may ache for a way through a period of uncertainty.

Perhaps you were frustrated as you sought to create something new because of the looming gap between where you were and where you wanted to be. Did the prospect of creating over again overwhelm you or paralyze you with fear? Was it easier to drift aimlessly than to engage in the process of renewal?

The main point of sharing my story is to let you know that whatever circumstances you find yourself in, you can improve upon them. Rest assured that there is a process. It may not be dramatic. In fact, it can be incredibly simple, even mundane. It may work overnight or take a fair amount of time. You may not even recognize that anything is happening until you are able to look back and see how far you have come. It would be easier for me to summarize what is possible when you undertake the creative process if our results were extremely dramatic. After all, you may be looking for the fade to black on a movie with all the loose ends tied up in a bow, while my own life is still a work in progress.

Having shared my story and the creative process with you, now what? How can I help you live this experience for yourself? Why will you be able to look back at my story as an example of the creative principles at work and begin to apply them for yourself?

If I were with you, you might never hear this story. It would all be part of who I am, an inner resource to draw upon if it would benefit you. Centered in my relationship with my subconscious, I would be watching and listening for insights, revelations, or new connections to help you deal with a perceived problem.

My days are filled with such conversations. They come in all shapes and sizes. If it's a problem that can be resolved with a procedure, we talk it through. We brainstorm for a creative solution. Some of my most enjoyable moments are when we are pushing the envelope of what we know how to do and what we have yet to discover. Our process is not about what cannot be done, but rather why we are able to do this.

These creative exchanges energize me. In contrast, working around budgetary limitations may feel more disheartening, but still yield surprises and even more creative potential to develop.

Emotional stress and strain among coworkers is common. There is a dynamic interplay of individuals and group that is injected into the daily rhythm of a show's structure and habit force. Emotions can energize or the reverse, serving to enhance or impede the work at hand. To keep all the creative juices flowing on a daily basis, it helps to acknowledge a problem and individual feelings, and then turn their attention from the negative to a positive solution. You may not always understand the circumstances or dynamics being created around you by your own actions or attitude. The goal will be to mutually discover a way to reconnect with others instead of allowing a wedge to develop, adjusting the focus from victim to proactive solution and positive intervention.

As I look around my current situation, I am surrounded by a version of my dream. Every day I get to feel what it is like to help others create. As we encounter new situations each day that lead to workable and creative solutions, I am reminded that we are never finished. The show is a fully functional example of my center, even if it is not exactly what I envisioned. I feel as if I am experiencing a version of the center—much as Peter and I felt about our small ranch when we first learned that we would need something bigger and set out to resolve the contrast. So, too, I now feel as if this is the leading edge of my work in the creative workplace. Do I know how it will unfold or how far I will get? Not yet. I only know what appears as the next-presented thing.

Allowing the vision to unfold is part of the process. Looking at my milestone map, I note my progress from the original book outline and my blog to being a published author. It reminds me that what I am living now attracts how the center's future manifestation will unfold. It is a good time to recommit to getting the word out to anyone who needs or wants to create.

It's my belief that we are all creative beings and that your awareness of the creative process will help you and that you can benefit from my experience more quickly if we begin dialoguing about the process in a healing and useful way.

Consider the power of questions. Watch, and if you catch yourself thinking negative thoughts or asking negative questions, flip your thinking. Ask only positive questions.

Apply the principles. Use the power of your mind—the creative thought process—every day. Let it begin with a question. If you do, you will find a powerful way to face crises, improve your life, and achieve your goals. Ask and you can receive.

Ask why you are so happy and so blessed. When all the outer trappings are removed, what would we like to feel: happy, blessed, love, joy, well-being, accomplishment, serenity? If we want to attract these feelings, this is a good place to start asking in order to allow the means to arrive. Choosing the right order of the questions is less important than asking whichever question inspires and gives you hope that you can feel better.

Why do you want to create or change something in your life? Why are you experiencing a contrast? The desire for change and the willingness to act provide the impetus to persist toward a goal. Where do you feel the sharpest contrast? Where do you feel the best?

How will moving toward your goal make you feel? What has to happen to make this change? What one thing could you do right now that would help you feel the way you want to feel? As I contemplate a day before moving into its activities, I ask for at least one thing that I can do today to move me closer to my goal.

Unsure about what you want or which solutions feel best for you? Now is a good time to ask for a positive solution. How will you feel when you eliminate the sticking points? If your mind is filled with negative thoughts like doubt, fear, or self-condemnation when you think about pursuing a goal, turn your thinking around in order to find the positive questions to ask. Play with the solutions that come to mind. Do some ideas have priority over others? Do some come up repeatedly? Which ones make you feel better? Why? Are they affecting something else that needs to change?

Ask for a next step and then take action. Even one action moves you toward a desired result. Deciding to take action as soon as insights or opportunities present is important. Decision activates the will to act. It energizes. Indecision stops us. Even the action of my daily routine supports the plan and helps foster belief, both consciously and subconsciously, as I express gratitude and affirm. In time, we begin to see the first actions that move us toward our goals so that we can get out of our own way and "just do it."

* Ask for clarity on your longer-term vision and purpose. Each time we seek to deliberately create anything, we first need to define a purpose, vision, or goal. You want to know why you want something, the way you want to feel when you have it, and have an awareness of what you can do right now to feel that way. Without a goal, we have no clear

sense of direction and may feel stuck, even depressed. Once we have defined our target, we get clear on where we want to go and move on to the next steps to achieve it. We can focus.

* *Why do you know where to place your focus? Ask for a plan you can lay out.* What are the next steps? Is there a long-term path to your accomplishments? Take an inventory of the ingredients you already have in your environment. I find it is so much fun to use my imagination to visualize the end results and then learn everything I can to develop a preliminary plan, preferably written or drawn out, that defines what has to happen in order for my vision to manifest. Without a plan, it is easy to get distracted or take a wrong turn without even knowing it. With a plan, you are able to focus and do the one thing you can do right now to move closer to your goals.

Once we have a vision, we have already created what we want in our minds. The more detailed the vision, the easier it is to bring what we want into our physical lives. The key is to visualize what you want to experience and feel, then ask for it and give thanks for what you are about to receive. When you ask, believing in the possibility, resources and opportunities begin to appear. One of the best parts of my daily routine is to express gratitude, noticing what is working and what is happening that matches my vision. I ask regularly until I believe an idea is possible. Then, my thoughts and feelings move me to take action.

* *Ask for effective ways to manage your progress.* Keep a scorecard, find a mentor, or use some other method of accountability. The final ingredients, continuing to focus on the goal daily and persist in action, are important. When you lose focus, you lose track of your goals. The greatest challenge is to pay attention and keep your eye on the ball, especially if you do not see the end results in the immediate future. For me, the most effective technique has been to keep asking positive questions every day. It helps me to relax and let go while still pursuing a goal. As you focus on your goals, surround yourself with support systems to help you do whatever is required and keep at it.

* *Take the time to study the mind.* Come to understand how outdated paradigms interfere with your progress.

Become aware of what's stopping you and ask questions to resolve those blocks. If you are not taking action, afforming helps to determine what is stopping you. Write down all the reasons you identify—the excuses—for why you did not step into any needed action when you perceived it.

Follow up with ways you can overcome those ideas. Imagine them. Feel them in a mind movie. Keep repeating this process.

Persist. Keep asking. Keep feeling. Keep visualizing. Keep focused on your goal.

Ask why you are so successful as you celebrate the fruits of your creations. As we complete each creation, new ideas will emerge. So pause to enjoy each creation before moving around the creative circle again. The subconscious, our higher self, is linked to the heart and responds to your positive feelings to become a powerful force for your next creation. Being cognizant of these simple steps in the midst of my daily routines is plenty. The reward will be the flash of insight bringing vision into reality. Suddenly, all the pieces come together to bring the insight into form. After a period of inactivity, the steps are clear and the resources are in hand.

The game in life is to recognize that we are always creating something new. We will never finish, because the essence of life force is to grow, expand, and create something new out of that which has gone before. As we contemplate a vision, we will identify contrasts that are developing. Each contrast represents a gap between our current experience and what we want to feel. Looking for the contrasts evidenced in our feelings, it becomes easier to look for actions we can take that can help us feel the way we want to feel in our current existence. For me, these actions become solutions to lighten my spirit in the moment. And when I lighten my spirit, amazing things happen. The result is that something new is continually emerging, along with new resources, new next steps, and new appreciation for what we have created.

CHAPTER 14

MOVING ON

Living in a creative environment, I am stunned by what has been accomplished in a year. I feel as if I have been given one God shot after another. It is as if my dream has magically appeared before my eyes in the process.

Our show caught the eye of the Television Academy, and the network renewed it. As all these events transpired, Noah St. John included a few paragraphs I wrote in his new book and interviewed me. My finances improved dramatically: my obligations reduced, my decimated savings restored, and I began to feel comfortable investing in my dreams again. I was able to see my family in Seattle every few months and improve our lifestyle.

As I look around my current situation, I am surrounded by a version of my dream. I head to the studio, where we tape the daily morning show, five days per week, for broadcast on a trusted network. We work in a campground of modular units, all focused on our studio space, which conveys a warm, creative, homelike environment, surrounded by gardens and lawns. Each production day, seventy people come together to create segments that help as many as thirty guests communicate ways to help others via their products, information, and services. My work is to support all these creative endeavors as if each participant were one of my perfect clients, to see ways to help each one live better while living in the pressure cooker of production. Every day in my supportive role, I get to feel what it is like to help others create. The show is a fully functional example of my vision, even if not exactly what I envisioned.

There are contrasts between the ideal vision and what I see around me, but it is so close, it takes my breath away. It is surprising because the studio is such a secular environment, where we have limited time to raise people's awareness of useful or creative work that is being done and there are few opportunities to guide or heal situations.

Still, I am so grateful that every day feels as if I already have the center. Perhaps I did not realize it when I began this journey, but it is not all about dreaming into the future. It is about living life and feeling the way you want to feel right now. You want to feel and hold the essence of what you are creating now. Daily life may intrude in the beginning, but we all have the power to turn our thoughts and feelings to what we would like instead. We can flip our thoughts. Thanks to the feelings generated by the show, my vision feels closer than ever, but I still have to live into it step-by-step, open to the next-presented thing, including strong contrasts, as revealed to me each day.

The most prominent decoration in my office is a huge vision board filled with colorful images of games and exercises set out to help me write. Occupying an entire wall, it is a place to hang evidence of accomplishments and reminders of upcoming activities, as well as a bigger-than-life version of the milestone map I carry with me to stay on track. While simultaneously writing in my spare time and working on the series, I have seen how integrated the creative thought process is within me. It may go by other names, like success principles, but as I read the words of Thomas Troward, the universe as creative consciousness resonates within me.

Creativity is my focus. It is my passion. Feeling the creative energy every day brings me joy. When engaged in the creative process, I feel energized and enthused. Seeing each day's show come together, I experience a sense of accomplishment. If an opportunity presents itself for me to dialogue with others in a healing way, so that people can apply the creative principles to improve their lives, then that is a very good day. In my current lifestyle, I make choices so that I can feel now what I expect to feel when I have the dream I am holding. Not only do these feelings infuse my workplace; they are also part of my daily activities for my personal life and vision of the future. I feel them in my normal routine: meditating, journaling, and writing on weekends; through my early morning collaboration as I align to the quantum waves of possibility I call source, receiving insights and experiencing occasional aha moments; again when I share my story and the creative principles in this book on my blogs or via the telephone and Skype. And I get an extra blessing of recognition and accomplishment when someone like Noah St. John includes my words in one of his books or interviews me over the telephone, and again when that talk catches the attention of one of my colleagues who reaches back to me.

Visualizing the future brings a rush of delight and anticipation, whether thinking about continuing my study of the creative process and having the opportunity to meet with others who share this passion or bringing joy and humor as I share my work, speaking, publishing and producing, or seeing the creative conference and retreat center grow from a dining room table and phone business to a presence at conferences, and ultimately, to a conference center dedicated to the communication of these spiritual principles and their practical application. I see its layout in my mind's eye and sketch it in my notebooks. The center comes to life first within myself. After that, it exists wherever I create the environment that permits me to live my purpose: sharing the creative process and supporting others in their creativity.

There is purpose in the process of holding the vision of millions of people realizing that their minds are each divine creative centers, always growing, expanding, and creating something new, proceeding out of their dominant thoughts, the dreams they hold, the passion they feel, and the actions they take. As the quantum physicists have been telling us, everything exists as a wave of possibility, waiting for our focus to collapse any idea into actuality right where we are today, in the immediate present.

Edgy anticipation accompanies thoughts about placing a gold star on my vision board soon. Looking at my milestone map, it is as if there is a magnifying glass on the milestone "write book." Preparing to move the glass reveals waves of possibility extending from it. There are still changes to make and marketing skills and operational elements to learn or delegate, yet it's time to put the finishing touches on my story.

Publishing will be a moment of truth as my emphasis shifts to interacting with others in a healing dialogue about the creative process. As part of raising awareness, there will be opportunities to guide people to apply these principles in their lives.

Imagine how I will feel, after years of personal growth and study, to acknowledge this shift. How did I move from not knowing to knowing, from unaware to aware, in order to reach this goal?

Have you ever heard the expression "You have to be it before you can have it"? While we are in the middle of the growing process, it is challenging to visualize just what that means. What do your senses tell you when you "are" something? We cannot help wondering if it is even possible to "be" before you have. Then suddenly, we come to the understanding that we have created what we envisioned. At first, we may not realize it. In fact, we may not become aware of the transformation until someone else tells us we have changed. Peter tells a story about his finally knowing that his work was valued when John Milius, the writer and director whom Peter holds in the highest personal esteem, told him how proud he was of Peter's accomplishments. People began to ask for his opinion. They sought him out. Only then did he accept that he had become a Western expert.

I call the moment beingness. Peter calls it contentment. It is the marvelous experience, after months (or years) of chasing the dream, when we have the impression that we have gained enough knowledge and systems to live it. We suddenly relax into a reality that this new creation has germinated.

Perhaps that is why gardening means so much to so many people. It is a microcosm of what happens creatively to each one of us. As the seed germinates, we do not see what is happening. It is almost always beneath the ground. Unseen to us, roots are sinking deeper into the soil. Then a tiny seedling shoots forth. We carefully nurture this fledgling, protecting it from harsh elements, providing the necessities for life. And gradually it changes from a seedling to a baby plant. New growth is evident. The plant will continue to grow, to send forth fruit, flowers, and seeds. As the gardeners of this new life, we will spend time nurturing its development, making sure it receives the correct amount of sunlight, water, and food, pruning away that which would inhibit or sap the strength of our plant, and shaping it into a strong and beautiful life-form.

Isn't it ironic that we build study into the action plan for our success, but may not allow time for becoming? There is a definite shift of energies. The stress reduces. We cease searching for the gimmick or tool that will catapult us forward. We are at the beginning of being our success.

What does that mean? It means that we hold the vision and make choices that support its achievement, but we stop chasing it. We live it. We persist in the actions, yet we no longer beat our head against the wall. The actions are just what we do as part of being who and what we are. We "suit up and show up for the next-presented thing" as it evolves. We let go of the compulsion to know and control the outcome. Life is. Life will. Energy is. Energy will. Do the work. Be. You will be rewarded in direct proportion to the service you provide others.

During much of the process, we have been focused on our personal achievement. With this new awareness, our focus shifts. We look outward to see how we can help others, rather than how we can help ourselves. For Peter, even as he continues to focus on his work, he has been writing and sharing his knowledge and experience of the Western, as well as his love of his animals, in children's books. In fact, a new *Travels of Oso and Neo* volume is due to arrive next week. As Peter continues his cross-country adventures with his traveling sidekick, Neo the dog, he too is aware of the game in life, the fun found in living one's passion, as he prepares a talk for the local community, sharing his expertise and love of the West, and applies his expertise in new movies that are in preparation.

The first season has wrapped, and it is only a matter of time before I will be getting into new rhythms: sharing this book, talking with others about their dreams and plans, nurturing and allowing these visions or something entirely new and unexpected to develop that will lead me on another turn of the spiral of life. There is well-being to be found as we play and create with others, mastering what is required for this particular part even as the next level emerges with an entirely new set of disciplines. I am living a creative process that began with a landslide. With joy, I accept where I am, and it's okay.

My journey has shown me how a vision can become a reality. Sharing the process is a passion that calls me forth from one space to another. The center is, at its simplest, a larger dream to take through the process. The first vague flickers of the next steps appear.

I am filled with the awareness that life is a process of joyful creation, which we first experience as conscious living, connected to a nonconscious reality that we may call our subconscious or supraconscious. It is not just a thought process. We may hold a vision in mind, but if we want to bring our dreams into the world, we need to bring the idea into a feeling state. It is not just a list or a picture. It is not just the words. It is the language of feeling that speaks to source energy.

How will you feel when you've made it? Imagine it. You have the job you've wanted, started the business, or developed the relationship you always dreamed about. Crisis and heartache have yielded to your desire to rebuild and recreate your life. Your play is on the stage.

Joy is found in the awareness that we can choose rainbows over ruins if that is where we find ourselves. We can embrace the path to our dreams through the process of moving from our vision to reality.

Now what? Even as you pause to smell the roses of success and accomplishment, a next step is revealed. It may be little more than a new idea, an introduction, or a chance meeting that suggests an opportunity as you approach completion. It becomes an invitation to ramp up your energies, evaluate your choices, and embrace a new destination. Change is the one thing we can count on. When we become that which we desire, there is always a new desire that calls us to become something more. Before you immerse yourself again, allow time to celebrate life's little successes. Enjoy them, and then begin to dream anew. Become willing to take that next step.

When the landslide happened, it broke up our habit patterns. Even though we wanted to restore normalcy, it had been life-altering. We could not go back. We could only embrace the change and do what we had to do to move forward.

In my vision, I see you being encouraged as you read my story. You see an example of someone living the creative principles. As you absorb the information, it becomes a guide that you can revisit as you move through the process yourself. It will inspire you to design your own journey, lay out your milestone map, discover your own breakthrough moment, and prepare to create the next spiral of your own tale. Knowing the value of contrasts in the process will prove helpful to you in reducing life's emotional roller coaster, providing focus, serenity, and strength with which to face life's challenges.

The reality is that we are never done. I have come to see that everything is part of the process of creating. It may be the life of our dreams or resolving even the smallest contrasts in order to improve our lifestyle. This creativity may be expressed through our work, our relationships, and a joyful sense of well-being. With each accomplishment, we return to the beginning.

Rainbows Over Ruins isn't just a story of learning to use the creative process in order to change my life. It's an opportunity to raise your awareness too. You can choose to engage your own creativity to improve your life as well. Let's start a dialogue. The perfect time is right now.

Find a quiet space in which to sit with me... to let ideas and images float by. Here, I still the conscious mind to align with quantum consciousness.

My hand is drawn to journal and mind map, allowing ideas to surface without judgment. There is no need to make sense or connection with them yet. The pause to center and identify with our true natures refines our sense of purpose, vision, and goals. A composite of mental vision, emotional belief, and physical actions stimulates results. As our minds ramble down this path, allow the proposed journey to unfold. It is all in the now.

A picture forms. It is a doppelganger standing in front of a group of people meeting to discuss a new creation. They are each contributing their ideas for its successful completion. On closer look, I see you are there too. We are creating together. I step to the board and begin to add details to the vision.

Allow the visualization images to flow. The scene shifts. With navigation charts and tools in our backpacks, we step into the boat that has carried me so far in my journey. Once again, I cast off the ropes and pull up the anchor holding us to the shore. I set the oars up, where there is no resistance, and take my seat, anticipating a "love whoosh" of desire that will propel us downstream. With one finger on the rudder, I am ready to set off on this most amazing, creative adventure. I am so grateful you have joined me on this ever-expanding journey. Having chosen rainbows over ruins, we are ready to create something even better.

Tell me, what would you like to create today?

APPENDIXES

APPENDIX I

AN OPENING MEDITATION ON BEGINNER'S MIND

A group of students patiently stand in line before a school. Each student speaks with a master before gaining entry.

The master asks one student, "What do you want?" "I do not know."

More experienced, the Wise One asks:

"If you did know, what would it be? Sit here outside and think of this." But the young person becomes distracted and chases bugs.

Again, the Wise One comes to him. "What do you want?" "I do not know."

And the Master says, "Dreams leave clues. Look around your life.

What surrounds you? Where have you spent your resources?"

And the young person is left to sit outside, pondering the clouds moving overhead.

The Wise One comes again. "Again, what do you want?" "I do not know."

"Then how will you know when you have it?"

The lines of students have continued to enter the ashram, but still the young student sits outside.

Again, the Wise One comes. "What do you want?" "I do not know."

"Then how will you know what to do to achieve it?"

Appendix II

The Creative Process

Are you recovering from a life crisis? Are you unsure of how to proceed? Are your emotions running wild so that you cannot think clearly? Have you experienced a great loss? As a result, do you desire to build something new?

Are you struggling with feelings of inadequacy, feeling stuck, confused that the choices you are making haven't yielded results yet? Are you looking to receive an education? Build a beautiful house with a view? Write a book? Create a garden? Improve your relationships or your health?

Everything begins with an idea. Whatever your dreams and desires, there is a creative process that you can follow to achieve them.

Suggested Materials

The process described in the previous pages includes several exercises that can be done repeatedly. Some are best performed daily. Others will be done once or repeated at various stages when it feels appropriate to do them again. It is suggested that you have:

A journal in which to record your thoughts and feelings; notebooks to jot down ideas, make drawings, and capture information in a visual format; and blank paper or whiteboards, where you can see your ideas and goals in symbols and pictures.

Index cards or small cards to carry with you or lay out around the house;

A recording device of some kind, if possible; and A CD player for audio support materials.

When beginning, you do not need to have all of these things; however, you will find them useful as you proceed. They do not have to be fancy or expensive. I find that when I find the materials I enjoy using, I tend to stick with them. No one else needs to see them, so please choose whatever provides you with a sense of creative joy and well-being when you use them.

The *deliberate creative process* exists to guide you as you develop what you want to create, map out where you want to go and what you'll need to do to get there, implement your plan, eliminate obstacles and blocks that are in your way, and celebrate when you get there. If you would like guidance, contact me at susan@susansherayko.com.

APPENDIX III

SUGGESTED READING AND ADDITIONAL RESOURCES

Abraham-Hicks © by Esther and Jerry Hicks. *Ask and It Is Given: Learning to Manifest Your Desires.* Carlsbad, CA: Hay House, 2004.

Abraham-Hicks © by Esther and Jerry Hicks. *The Astonishing Power of Emotions: Let Your Feelings Be Your Guide.* Carlsbad, CA: Hay House, 2007.

Assagioli, Roberto. *The Act of Will.* New York: Penguin Books, 1985.

Assaraf, John, and Murray Smith. *The Answer.* New York: Atria Paperback, 2008.

Babish, Rev. Barbara Marie. www.thewayoftherainbow.com.

Behrend, Genevieve. *Your Invisible Power.* Radford, VA: Wilder Publications, LLC, 2008.

Bolles, Richard. *What Color Is My Parachute?* Berkeley, CA: Ten Speed Press, 2011.

Briggs, Sondra. *Port Hueneme Beach Walks: My Path to Peace.* Port Hueneme, CA: Neshama Press, 2008.

Bristol, Claude M. *The Magic of Believing*. New York: Pocket Books, 1948.

Brothers, Dr. Joyce. *The Brothers System for Liberated Love and Marriage*. New York: P. H. Wyden, 1972.

Byrd, David. *The Language of Achievement*. Waco, TX: PCG Business, 2012.

Byrd, David, and Mark Smith. *Achievement: A Proven System for Next-Level Growth*. Waco, TX: PCG Business, 2010.

Byrne, Rhonda. *The Secret*. Hillsboro, OR: Beyond Words Publishing, 2006.

Cilley, Marla. *Sink Reflections*. New York: Bantam Dell, 2004.

Daly, Sandra Anne. *Pop Your Paradigms*. Scottsdale, AZ: Inkwell Productions, 2009.

Dyer, Wayne W. *There Is a Spiritual Solution to Every Problem*. New York: Harper Collins, 2001.

Goswami, Amit. *God Is Not Dead*. Charlottesville, VA: Hampton Roads Publishing Company, Inc., 2008.

Halvorsen, Dr. Heidi Grant. *Succeed: How We Can Reach Our Goals*. New York: The Penguin Group, 2010.

Hawkins, David R. *Power vs. Force: The Hidden Determinants of Human Behavior*. Carlsbad, CA: Hay House, 2002.

Hill, Napoleon. *The Master Key to Riches*. New York: Ballantine Press, 1965.

Hill, Napoleon. *Napoleon Hill's Original Law of Success*. New York: Jeremy P. Tarcher/Penguin, originally published in 1928.

Hill, Napoleon, and Ross Cornwall. *Think and Grow Rich: The Original Version, Restored and Revised*. Clemson, SC: The Mindpower Press, 2008.

Hoisington, T. J. *If You Think You Can*. North Fort Myers, FL: Aylesbury Publishing, LLC, 2005.

King, Vivian. *Being Here When I Need Me: An Inner Journey*. Findhorn, Scotland: Inner Way Productions, 1998.

Kiyosaki, Robert T. *The Business of the 21ˢᵗ Century*. Scottsdale, AZ: DreamBuilders, 2010.

Lechter, Sharon, and Greg S. Reid. *Three Feet from Gold*. New York: Sterling Publishing Co., Inc., 2009.

Maltz, Maxwell. *Psycho-Cybernetics*. Englewood Cliffs, NJ: Prentice-Hall, Inc., 1960.

Murphy, Dr. Joseph. *The Power of Your Subconscious Mind*. New York: Prentice Hall Press, 2008.

Murphy, Dr. Joseph. *Think Yourself Rich*. New York: Prentice Hall Press, 2001.

Olson, Jeff. *The Slight Edge*. Lake Dallas, TX: Success Books, 2005.

Proctor, Bob. *You Were Born Rich*. Scottsdale, AZ: LifeSuccess Productions, 2002.

Sheehy, Gail. *New Passages*. New York: Ballantine Books, 1996.

St. John, Noah. *The Book of Afformations*. Carlsbad, CA: Hay House, 2013.

Zukav, Gary. *The Dancing Wu Li Masters*. New York: Bantam Books, 1979.

Audio and Video Programs

Beckwith, Michael, Jack Canfield, and Bob Proctor. *The Science of Getting Rich*. Scottsdale, AZ: LifeSuccess Productions, 2007.

Gerard, Genevieve. *Meditations for Daily Joy: A Series of Awareness Meditations*. Huntington Beach, CA: Touch of the Soul, 2011. www. genevievegerard.com.

Proctor, Bob. *The Goal Achiever*. Scottsdale, AZ: LifeSuccess Productions, 2003.

Proctor, Bob. *Mission in Commission*. Scottsdale, AZ: LifeSuccess Productions, 2002.

Proctor, Bob. *Success Puzzle*. Scottsdale, AZ: LifeSucess Productions, 2003.

Proctor, Bob. *What to Do When It's Not Working*. Scottsdale, AZ: LifeSuccess Productions, 2005.

Proctor, Bob. *The Winner's Image*. Scottsdale, AZ: LifeSuccess Productions, 2002.

Proctor, Bob. *You Were Born Rich*. Scottsdale, AZ: LifeSuccess Productions, 2003.

Robert, Gerry. *The Millionaire Mindset: How Ordinary People Can Create Extraordinary Income*. Scottsdale, AZ: Life Success Publishing,2007.

Rohn, Jim. *The Art of Exceptional Living*. Niles, IL: Nightingale Conant, 1993.

Rohn, Jim. *Challenge to Succeed*. Lake Dallas, TX: Jim Rohn International: 1991–2008.

Home-Study Programs

St. John, Noah. *The Afformations System: The Missing Piece to Having Abundance*. Uniontown, Ohio: Success Clinic International, LLC: 2012. www.HavingAbundance.com.

St. John, Noah. *Power Habits Academy: The New Science for Making Success Automatic*. Uniontown, Ohio: Success Clinic International,LLC 2013. www.PowerHabitsAcademy.com.

Counseling

Psychosynthesis: To find a directory of centers and practitioners, go to http://two.not2.org/psychosynthesis/centers/index.htm.

Coaching Programs

Proctor, Bob – LifeSuccess Productions, 8900 E. Pinnacle Peak Road, Scottsdale, Arizona 85255, Tel: 480-657-6336.

Wilson, Sharon – Coaching from Spirit, LLC, Drums, Pennsylvania Tel: 888-542-2250. www.coachingfromspirit.com.

Twelve-Step Books

Hazelden Foundation, www.hazelden.org.

The Abraham-Hicks Materials

Abraham-Hicks, www.AbrahamHicks.com, contact number 830-755-2299.

More from Susan Sherayko at:

Her coaching at: www.embracepositivechange.com

Her course at: www.dreamroadmap.com

Her website: www.SusanSherayko.com

Her podcasts at: Train Your Brain Claim Your Power on Spotify

XOTV.me/Rebuilding Your Life Radio

Everyday Happiness at Waterberg Stereo 104.9 in Limpopo, South Africa

Social media at: Twitter.com/ssherayko

Facebook.com/Susan Sherayko

Ssherayko.wordpress.com

Youtube.com Channel: Susan Sherayko

Instagram: rainbowsoverruins

www.ingramcontent.com/pod-product-compliance
Lightning Source LLC
Chambersburg PA
CBHW051151120626
46547CB00012B/1040